003431

S0-BSE-313

Learning Resources Center
Collin County Community College District
SPRING CREEK CAMPUS
Plano, Texas 75074

DATE DUE

SEP 0 5 1988	
NOV 1 9 1990	
FEB. 25 1994	
APR 1 8 1995	
ILL 7-13-98	

BRODART, INC.   Cat. No. 23-221

EARLY ARCHITECTURE IN NEW MEXICO

EARLY ARCHITECTURE IN NEW MEXICO

Bainbridge Bunting

UNIVERSITY OF NEW MEXICO PRESS   Albuquerque

Library of Congress Cataloging in Publication Data

Bunting, Bainbridge.
    Early architecture in New Mexico.

    Bibliography: p.
    Includes index.
    1. Architecture—New Mexico—History. I. Title.
NA730.N38B86   720.9789   76-21511
ISBN 0-8263-0424-9
ISBN 0-8263-0435-4 pbk.

Copyright © 1976 by the University of New Mexico Press. All rights reserved.
Manufactured in the United States of America. Library of Congress Catalog
Card No. 76-21511. International Standard Book Number (clothbound) 0-8263-0424-9
International Standard Book Number (paperbound) 0-8263-0435-4
Third paperbound printing 1984

to

JOHN GAW MEEM

whose buildings and whose efforts for preservation
have contributed so much to the architectural
heritage of New Mexico.

This book is based upon three lectures delivered to the Historic Preservation Division of the Graduate School of Architecture and Planning of Columbia University in 1973. They were part of a series, planned and coordinated by Professor James M. Fitch, dealing with the morphological development of American vernacular architecture. The series was made possible by grants from the Edgar Kaufmann Charitable Foundation of Pittsburgh and the J. M. Kaplan Fund of New York City.

CONTENTS

LIST OF ILLUSTRATIONS

1

INTRODUCTION

Man has been constructing permanent shelters in New Mexico for more than 1,500 years; for over half that time his buildings have been large and substantial. An account of his building activity carries one back to primitive pithouses which appear as early as A.D. 350. Construction of multiunit dwellings above ground began about A.D. 700. Given such antiquity and continuity, it is surprising that so little is left today in the way of ancient buildings. In Indian pueblos structures of genuine antiquity can be counted on one hand, and include Taos Pueblo and fragments of buildings in a few other places. Of thirty surviving churches which were built before 1800 in Indian and Spanish communities, less than a dozen retain a convincing colonial appearance. Of Spanish civil and domestic building even less remains except for foundations and portions of early walls incorporated into later buildings. This is true even of the Palace of the Governors, begun in 1610 in Santa Fe. Although an adobe wall built in 1700 is not very different from one erected in 1900, the appearances of completed buildings from those dates vary considerably. It is therefore misleading to suggest that just because a building was begun long ago, its present aspect is representative of that early date, an impression too often conveyed by tourist books attempting to underscore the antiquity of the area.

A historian obsessed with categories and dates can divide New Mexican history since man settled into established communities and began to build shelters that were more or less permanent into perhaps a dozen periods. The names and dates used for the early periods are borrowed from anthropologists who defined them at a historic conference held at Pecos in 1927. Later classifications, which attempt to distinguish the stages of change since American occupation, are this author's. It will be useful at the outset to define these periods and to provide a minimum of historic background.

The general names for the prehistoric Indians inhabiting the Southwest are Hohokam, Mogollon, and Anasazi. It is the Anasazi, those people living in the Four Corners area of Utah, New Mexico, Arizona, and Colorado, who will concern us here. The Anasazi are divided into two groups by archaeologists, Basket Maker and Pueblo, which differ in certain material culture traits as a consequence of changes in ways of life through time. The Basket Makers represent the earlier portion of the Anasazi continuum. To standardize nomenclature and to identify certain differences in life styles, Basket Maker culture is divided into two parts: Basket Maker II, from about A.D. 1 to 350 and Basket Maker III, 350 to 700. Their name derives from the fact that they were excellent weavers of baskets and other items of fiber such as sandals and bags. The earliest Basket Makers lacked pottery, used the *atlatl,* or spear thrower, to propel stone-tipped spears, lived mostly in natural rock shelters, and made a living by hunting and gathering coupled with elementary farming. By 350 important additions to their culture had occurred: they had learned to use the bow and arrow, added pottery making to their skills, become more proficient as farmers—raising corn, beans, and squash—and had commenced to build pithouses outside the confines of caves.

The changes that evolved by A.D. 700 are numerous enough to cause the latter part of Anasazi culture to be identified as Pueblo, a name given it and its members by the first Spanish explorers who found the indigenous population settled in permanent towns, or pueblos. Pueblo culture is divided into five periods, but it should be understood that the dates assigned the periods cover the entire Anasazi area and do not account for cultural advances and lags in specific localities. Pueblo I extends from approximately 700 to 900; Pueblo II, 900 to 1050; Pueblo III, 1050 to 1300; Pueblo IV, 1350 to about 1700; and Pueblo V, 1700 to recent times.

During the Pueblo I and Pueblo II periods, villages of pithouses evolved into small communities with rows of contiguous, flat-roofed houses built above ground of poles and mud, and then into small towns in which the rectilinear house units were built of stone masonry and sometimes were multistoried. The kiva, an underground ceremonial chamber, became an integral part of each settlement. Advances in the arts and crafts, particularly in pottery making, led to regional specializations. Pueblo III is the Classic period, the apogee of Anasazi culture, when large numbers of people occupied towns of considerable size and social complexity flourished. Peaks were reached in architectural and engineering achievements, in agricultural accomplishments (including water control systems for irrigating arid lands), in in the manufacture of goods, pottery vessels, tools, and ornaments, and in the trade of items both within and outside the Anasazi realm.

As a result of numerous factors including pressure from nomadic peoples, depletion of resources, and perhaps social unrest, the heavily populated northern centers of the Anasazi were abandoned around 1300 and over a period of several generations the inhabitants migrated southward to new sites along the Rio Grande and its tributaries or to locations in west central New Mexico and east central Arizona. The Pueblo IV period not only witnessed a population shift but was marked by cultural regression. Practically all Anasazi activities declined from their previous levels of accomplishment. It was during this time, however, that most pueblos that have survived to the present were established.

Some of these Pueblo IV communities appear to have been moving toward a cultural renaissance when Francisco Vásquez de Coronado led the first Spanish expedition into the Southwest in 1540. Although Christianization of the Indians began even before permanent Spanish colonization in 1598, contact with the Europeans was not close enough to cause marked cultural changes until about 1700, after the return of the Spaniards to the area following the Pueblo Revolt of 1680–93. During the Revolt, Pueblo culture suffered serious dislocations, including a marked population decline due to war, disease, and migrations to join other Indian groups. Pueblo V culture has been progressively affected by outside influences, first Spanish and then American. The rate of change has so augmented since World War II, with the advent of the automobile and television, that one might now speak of present-day Indian culture as Pueblo VI or even post-Pueblo.

Following several unauthorized and impermanent attempts at colonization, the Spaniards finally established themselves in New Mexico in 1598. In 1610 Santa Fe was founded as the administrative center while small groups of colonists appropriated agricultural sites near existing pueblos along the northern reaches of the Rio Grande and its tributaries. Franciscan friars were recruited from Mexico so that Christianization among the Indians was carried out. Along with Christianity, the Spanish introduced the horse and other livestock (sheep, cows, and pigs), important agricultural products (wheat and other cereals, fruit trees, and many vegetables), the wheel, gunpowder, and metal tools into New Mexico. They did not, however, find the mineral wealth they had hoped for (though there are deposits in the area), and Spanish migration to New Mexico was slow. Before the Revolt of 1680 the Spanish population numbered only about 2,800. A few influential individuals procured grants of land from the crown, but most Spaniards led a hand-to-mouth existence. Based on material remains found in the excavations of some seventeenth-century sites, it is often hard to distinguish between Spanish and Indian communities. Since so little economic profit could be derived from the province, the crown's principal interest was the Christianization of the Indians. To this end the Spanish government supported the friars' missionary activity and supplied such materials as they required. In pursuance of this, each friar charged with gathering a new congregation of Indians and building a church, was issued a standard "building kit." The small kit contained tools and materials for building, and included everything from axes and spades to nails and hinges. A supply train was established that triennially made the hazardous 1,500-mile trip from Mexico City to Santa Fe bringing essential equipment and cult objects. The friars laboring in isolation in remote pueblos were left to their own devices, and their work of conversion as well as the construction of churches was largely a matter of persuasion. The crown paid considerably less attention to Spanish settlers, many of whom were concentrated in Santa Fe under the protection of the royal governor and a garrison that sometimes was very small.

When the Spaniards returned to New Mexico in 1693 after quelling the Pueblo Revolt, the tenor of life and the structures they built were similar to those of the seventeenth century. New centers of Spanish settlement in the Rio Grande Valley were established, such as Santa Cruz (1695) and Albuquerque (1706), while somewhat later, grants of land were given to groups of impoverished families willing to take up residence in places on the frontier like Las Trampas (1751). These outposts served to ward off attacks by nomadic Indians—Apache, Comanche, Ute, and Navajo—who had begun to harass both Spanish and Pueblo settlements in the Rio Grande Valley. However, the level of subsistence was so minimal as to leave little margin for experimentation or chance. The colonists held on by their fingernails. The result was a cultural crystallization. The language, for example, retained seventeenth-century usages, and technology did not advance. Although the area possessed excellent clay, such simple processes as brick- and tile-making were never developed. The architectural form of the church, introduced in 1610, was repeated without substantive change in 1816 (Chimayó) and even as late as 1890 (Sto. Domingo). Trade with non-Spanish areas was forbidden by the crown so that foreign goods had to be imported through Mexico City. By the time they reached New Mexico, they cost many times their original value. New Mexico remained a most remote and isolated place.

As long as Spain controlled her colonies in America, the missions were supplied by the crown with friars and materials, but with the advent of Mexican independence in 1821, this support was discontinued. The new administration in Mexico City was too preoccupied with immediate problems to bother about remote New Mexico, especially since the latter was too poor to contribute men or money to support the shaky government. In 1834, the mission stations were secularized and the Franciscan friars forced to relinquish their role as ministers and protectors of the Indians to secular priests (those not bound by monastic rule) under the jurisdiction of the Bishop of Durango (Mexico). Most friars returned to monasteries in Mexico or Spain, and only two Franciscan brothers were still serving here when Father Jean Baptiste Lamy arrived in 1850. Like the national government, the Mexican church was too beset by financial and administrative problems—as well as by a shortage of priests—to send to New Mexico either supplies or replacements for the dismissed Franciscans. As a result the province was left very much to its own devices during both the War of Independence (1810–20) and the Mexican period (1820–46). By 1850 there were only fourteen clerics in the entire province. It was during these decades of isolation that New Mexicans learned to minister to their own needs and developed some of their most characteristic institutions and art forms. The Penitente brotherhood came into prominence to care for the spiritual needs of a population that in many instances was without priests. And this was the great period of *santeros* (makers of religious images) who painted *retablos* (pictures) and fashioned *bultos* (statues) for church, Penitente, or individual use. Anglo-American penetration of New Mexico began with the establishment of trade over the Santa Fe Trail in 1821. Prior to that, American or French merchants imprudent enough to venture into the area often found themselves under arrest, and their goods confiscated by the Spanish officials. Amounting to no more than $75,000 in 1825, the trade along the Trail had grown to $5,000,000 by 1855.

With the outbreak of the Mexican War the province was promptly occupied by General Stephen Watts Kearny (in the summer of 1846) and in 1848 the area was officially annexed as a United States territory. The subsequent Territorial period divides into three short phases: early, 1846–65; middle, 1865–85; and late, 1880–1912.

Administrative and economic changes were instituted soon after annexation. An American governor and officials were sent to Santa Fe. United States troops remained in New Mexico both to insure acquiescence of the Mexican population and to control the movements of the nomadic, non-Pueblo Indians who for a century had harassed the area. To the latter end a series of military outposts such as Forts Union, Burgwin, Stanton, and Wingate were established. Equally important, the Vatican decided in 1850 to sever New Mexico from the Diocese of Durango and place it under the reform leadership of Father Jean Baptiste Lamy, a French-born priest who, in 1853, became the Bishop of New Mexico. Suspicious of some of the clergy who carried over from the Mexican administration, Lamy brought in from the Midwest priests and members of several religious orders (the Christian Brothers, the Sisters of Loretto, and eventually a number of Jesuits) to staff churches and found schools. Many of these people were of French origin, and they, as well as the bishop, sought to reform and revitalize the church. Technological innovations were not long in appearing and soon Santa Fe Trail merchants were supplying the local market with new essentials—window glass, nails, and metal hardware. Despite these innovations, the architecture of the territory did not change much before the outbreak of the Civil War. Then building slumped, civilian trade diminished, and most of the army units were called east.

The middle Territorial phase begins with the end of the Civil War and continues until after the arrival of the railroad in 1880 when the economic penetration of the area was carried forward in force. Efforts were made to bring the three populations—Mexican, Indian, and American—together under a single set of laws. Land titles were scrutinized and substantiated and taxes imposed under the American system. Along with the new legal system came a good deal of crooked dealing to the detriment of Mexican and Indian proprietors unfamiliar with the intricacies of American law. For a while trade was equally divided between Mexican and American merchants, though increasingly the Americans got the upper hand. Prominent among the latter were a large number of Jewish merchants who had immigrated from Germany. Inasmuch as some nomadic Indians had taken advantage of the absence of federal troops during the war as an opportunity to resume their depredations, military posts were reactivated and rebuilt in a more permanent and architecturally impressive form. During this same period large numbers of Navajos were rounded up and exiled (1864–68) to Fort Sumner in eastern New Mexico. This was the period when the so-called Territorial style of architecture was at its height.

The late Territorial phase covers the thirty-two-year interval between the arrival of the railroad in 1880 and the achievement of statehood in 1912. It was a period of enormous change and relative prosperity. Railroad construction created jobs, built boom towns, and brought a flood of new inhabitants to the area. It also made possible the sale and export of wool, hides, grains, and minerals produced in New Mexico. Clearing the mountainous regions of marauding Indians had opened these areas to prospectors and the resultant silver mining enjoyed a brief prosperity. The state's substantial copper resources, however, were not exploited on a large scale until after 1900, and large deposits of coal were principally worked for the benefit of the railroad. Although manufactured goods from the Midwest were now brought within easy reach of towns along the railroad, mountainous areas remained relatively unaffected by this supply until after World War I.

Statehood in itself caused no immediate changes. Even before 1912 towns along the railroad such as Albuquerque, East Las Vegas, or Deming pretty much resembled small towns anywhere in the Midwest, while towns like Taos and Santa Fe retained a marked regional character. A significant cultural change in some communities came about indirectly as the result of World War I, which forced American artists and expatriates to give up residence in Europe. A number of these discovered the picturesque quality and relative economy of New Mexico, and in the course of time well-known art communities grew up in Taos and Santa Fe. The area drew additional visitors as a summer and a health resort. Throughout this period New Mexico remained a place apart, unique because of its blend of Indian, American, and Mexican cultures. Not until World War II did New Mexico climb into the twentieth century. A mixed blessing, this was accomplished by the building of military bases in the area, huge expenditures of money for atomic research at Los Alamos and Albuquerque, the channeling of transcontinental automobile traffic on Highway 66 (now I–40), and the establishment of air routes which included Albuquerque as a major terminal. In the process most New Mexican cities and towns have come to resemble American communities anywhere and "progress," aided by urban renewal, now erodes such traces of individuality as had survived. The standard of living has come up—though still not to national averages—but the visual character of communities has deteriorated.

The reason for the absence of extant ancient structures in New Mexico lies in the nature of the material of which many were built, adobe. Adobe, an Arabic word, or even possibly one that derives from an ancient Egyptian root, describes a mixture of sand and clay combined in proper proportions so that an optimum hardness is achieved. If the mixture contains too much sand, the adobe is soft and weathers poorly; if too much clay, it cracks and is useless as a building material. Adobe is, nevertheless, an easy substance with which to build and in many locations the only one available. It also possesses characteristics that recommend it, even to modern builders, such as economy and good thermal and sound insulation. It is, however, a poor material as far as durability is concerned. This is because the substance is thoroughly organic—"organic" in a molecular sense if not in the personal way Frank Lloyd Wright chose to redefine the term. That an adobe structure is part of the earth from which it is formed is indicated by the forest of weeds so often found sprouting from the roof of a New Mexico house (fig. 1). As soon as a building is constructed it begins to disintegrate and requires continuous repair. As a rule of thumb, one estimates that given twenty years of neglect, an adobe structure is beyond the point where it is worth repairing; by then it is simply easier to start over. Add to this the ease with which an adobe

1 Typical earth-covered roof with drains in the form of wooden canales.

building can be remodeled, and one understands why so little remains of its original form.

Why is adobe construction so fugitive, so transitory? This, of course, is because adobe, almost as hard as stone when dry, softens when exposed for too long a time to moisture. There are three areas where an adobe building is extremely vulnerable. The first danger point is the roof, which in New Mexico traditionally consisted of a wooden covering overlaid with 4 to 6 inches of earth. The way to repair a leaky roof is to locate the place where the water trickles through, get a bucket of earth from the yard, climb to the roof, and dump the mud on the trouble spot. This generally does the trick, but it also means that in the course of time the earth covering builds up to considerable depths of great weight. Such quantities of moist earth encourage rot in the beams that support it, and about every 75 to 100 years the entire roof has to be replaced. Although we have buildings going back to 1610, or to the early 1700s, their roofs have been entirely replaced several times.

Another constant trouble spot is roof drains which carry off rain water. When it rains, the clay soil covering the roof is quickly saturated and the rest of the rain must run off. Thus the earth is graded to a low spot where a *canale*, or roof drain is provided to throw the water clear of the wall. When the canale is not kept in repair, water gets under it and trickles down the face of the wall causing erosion. After a couple of good rains, the wall under a defective roof drain simply dissolves (fig. 2).

The third critical area is the groundline. Southwestern rainfalls are not so heavy that beating rains wash away the walls. (In Albuquerque the average yearly rainfall is about seven inches, at higher altitudes more.) The trouble occurs at the groundline where capillary action (the result of surface tension that makes liquids in contact with solid matter rise) causes the adobe wall to become damp and soft in a zone above ground level; when too soft, the wall simply sloughs away. Since there is more ground moisture outside than inside a roofed building, erosion of the outside surface of an adobe wall is far more pronounced than on the inside. Thus whenever an adobe building has collapsed, its walls, undermined from the outside, have always fallen outwards.

Despite the scarcity of structures retaining their original features, considerable visual data remain in one form or another that indicate how early buildings were constructed and what they looked like. Archaeological excavations provide information on plans and early building techniques, and some Indian villages even today still retain the flat roofs, multistoried composition, and contiguous alignment of early times. This is especially true of communities like Acoma and Santa Ana where the old pueblos are retained for ceremonial purposes even though the people have moved to new homes in locations nearer their fields. Evidence can also be derived from edifices erected as late as 1880 in areas where early building techniques and architectural solutions were retained because of

2 Wall eroded by defective canale.

isolation. Finally, there are photographs made in the last decades of the nineteenth century which record early structures then standing. Drawing on such diverse sources, it is possible to reconstruct the form and character of the area's early architecture.

The word "adobe" refers both to the material and to the sunbaked bricks into which the material is formed. The technique of shaping mud into bricks was brought to New Mexico by the Spaniards, who had learned it from the Arabs, who, through innumerable intermediaries, had got it from ancient Mesopotamia. Adobe as a material, however, had been used in the Southwest long before Spaniards arrived. Here the Indians had a way of forming the mud into long, low bands which we call "puddled adobe" (fig. 3). It resembles "pisé," or

3 Pueblo IV puddled adobe walls at Pot Creek, excavated by Fort Burgwin Research Center.

rammed-earth construction, except that here the bands of mud from 15 to 20 inches high were laid without the aid of wooden forms. The mud was sufficiently stiff when put in place to permit the builders to compact and shape it by hand. The technique was laborious and slow as each band had to dry thoroughly (because clay shrinks as it dries) before the next one could be added, a process that may have required several months per layer. An examination of puddled adobe walls found in excavations reveals, in addition to horizontal joints between the layers, thin vertical cracks where the band had shrunk as it dried. These excavations also show that Indian builders were not aware of the structural advantages of bonding walls at corners or where they intersect one another. But inasmuch as adobe had no tensile or shearing strength, such bonding would have provided little protection against foundation settlement. Considering that they may have supported several upper stories, these puddled walls—hardly ever more than 12 inches wide—are surprisingly thin. As a result structural failure must have been common, especially when thin, overloaded walls were further weakened by erosion. An exception is the great structure at Casa Grande, Arizona, where puddled walls four feet thick rose to an estimated height of forty feet. A more typical example of puddled construction in the Rio Grande Valley is a group of rooms still standing at Picurís Pueblo (fig. 4). Now almost abandoned, Picurís, which lies some twenty miles distant from Taos, was one of the largest pueblos when Spaniards came into the area in the sixteenth century. The remaining rooms formed the core of a housing block about which later rooms had accreted. Later the block gradually wasted away so that today only a few center rooms of puddled construction remain.

Probably because the shaping of adobe into brick makes for fast and easy

4   Pueblo IV puddled adobe masonry, Picuris Pueblo. Photograph, 1899, by A. C. Vroman
(No. 2074 in the National Anthropological Archives, Smithsonian Institution).

construction, this method was used extensively by the Indians. The technique of forming adobe brick is simple: a stiff, doughlike mixture of earth and water is packed into a rectangular frame of wood which is then lifted off leaving the mud on the ground to dry (fig. 5). In good drying weather two days are sufficient to stiffen the mud block so it can be turned on end. Within a week it is hard enough to be stacked for curing, which may require an additional month. Bricks made today measure approximately 10 x 14 x 4 inches and weigh about 35 pounds, which is about as heavy a unit as a mason can conveniently handle. Examination of early buildings indicates, however, that dimensions have varied with time and location. Bricks in the exposed walls of a seventeenth-century church, like that at Hawikuh, are long and narrow (about 12 x 18 x 3 inches) and laid with mortar joints almost as thick as the adobe itself. This is much thicker than the half-inch joints used today. The present standard brick thickness of 4 inches is undoubtedly due to the availability of 2 x 4-inch lumber used to make the mold (*adobero*) in which the brick is cast. The mixture of clay and sand for mortar is the same as that for brick.

5   Making adobe bricks, Zuñi Pueblo. Photograph attributed to A. C. Vroman (No. 47,729 in the National Anthropological Archives, Smithsonian Institution).

In the Rio Arriba region, along the northern reaches of the Rio Grande which lie at a high elevation and have more rain, adobe makers add straw to the mixture because it aids primarily in drying. In the Rio Abajo (the lower Rio Grande Valley around Albuquerque) straw is not usually added. There, however, builders alternately employ *terrones*. Terrón is sod with fairly deep roots, spaded up in long, rectangular chunks and dried in exactly the same way as adobe brick. The root system serves as a bond and aids in the drying process. It appears that terrón was not known in pre-Spanish times, and even later its use was restricted to localities with bottomland where sod was plentiful. Because adobes are heavy, and transportation was sparse, builders in early times always manufactured their brick as near as possible to the building site.

In addition to adobe, puddled or fashioned into brick, two other materials were utilized by Indians and Spaniards to construct edifices: stone and jacal. In certain parts of New Mexico nature provides outcroppings of ledge stone that make excellent building material. Pieces from these outcroppings were generally used just as they were broken by nature since the Indians had no metal tools for trimming stone. (In some localities during the Classical period, 1050–1300, builders shaped stone accurately with stone hammers and erected walls of extraordinary beauty; see fig. 6.) The ledge rock was laid in a mortar of adobe mud. Such construction weathered much better than ordinary adobe work, especially when the mud mortar was forced into the joints only after the stone was laid. If constructed in that way, the wall was not subject to settlement which

12

6 Stone masonry at Pueblo Bonito; examples of three of the four periods of construction. The white lines bound a two-foot-square section.

otherwise took place when mud in the joints washed out. The greatest use of stone is in villages located in the Four Corners area and in the mountains east of the Rio Grande Valley.

Jacal construction involves setting vertical members of wood in the ground at short intervals and filling between them with mud. It was used by prehistoric Indians, Spaniards, and nineteenth-century builders in very different ways. In Indian hands the vertical members were poles woven together with brush and coated on both sides with a layer of adobe plaster (fig. 7). Buildings of such light construction were used as temporary storage buildings or animal shelters. In Pueblo I times, the Anasazi used jacal construction extensively for their houses. Occasionally these have been preserved in cliff dwellings where the flimsy construction was protected from moisture by a ledge overhanging the alcove in which the dwelling was built. Spanish colonial builders employed jacal in storage buildings and animal shelters also, and sometimes for non-bearing partitions within a masonry house. A quite different type of jacal, using logs of fair size and employed in the latter part of the nineteenth century, will be discussed later.

7 Lightweight jacal construction used for a twentieth-century storage building in southern New Mexico.

No matter what material the wall was made of, roof construction of traditional New Mexico houses was very much the same. A system of horizontal beams was supported by the walls and overlaid with earth which shed rain and provided insulation. The span of the roof differed in Indian and Spanish buildings inasmuch as the former, having only stone axes, had greater difficulty felling large trees for beams. Though indigenous builders could procure very large beams when occasion demanded, as for the support of large kiva roofs, in ordinary domestic construction they generally employed beams 4 to 8 inches in diameter; the Spaniards, equipped with metal tools, preferred logs with diameters of 10 to 12 inches. Thus, as a general rule, the clear spans of Indian rooms are shorter, ranging from 6 to 14 feet; those in Spanish dwellings are generally about 15 feet. There are, of course, exceptions since pueblos or Spanish communities farther from the mountains sometimes made do with lighter roof timbers. Construction of buildings for the first Anglo-Americans in the area differed little from those of the Spanish.

With the span restricted by the size of available roof timbers, the dimensions of a room could only be varied in one direction, lengthwise. The consistent use of uniform spans within a building creates a modular quality in the architecture. The module is the more apparent because roofs are flat. A paucity of window and door openings in early structures likewise emphasized the sense of geometry. Thus a community appeared to be made up of a series of blocks or modular units which could be composed in a variety of ways and which possess considerable aesthetic interest. Although the module of the Indian community was somewhat smaller than that employed in a Spanish or early American structure, all three expressions share a basic similarity.

CHAPTER ONE

The difference between communities of these three cultures was the way in which the modular units were composed. The Indians tended to pile their cubes into irregular pyramids, like a pile of sugar lumps (as at Taos Pueblo), though they sometimes also grouped them around a court as in the pueblos at Frijoles or Chaco canyons (figs. 8, 9). The Spaniards arranged their cubes in a single file to form a series of rooms (fig. 10). Sometimes these contiguous units carried around the sides of an open court or, on a village scale, enclosed a fortified plaza. The early Americans decentralized their communities and dispersed individual living units through the countryside. The point to emphasize here is that from 700 down to 1880, a basic unity persisted because of the modular method of building; differences between communities of the three cultures were primarily a matter of how the modules were composed. This rather extraordinary conservatism prevailed despite cultural changes because the poverty and isolation of New Mexico permitted little technological progress prior to the construction of the railroad into the Rio Grande Valley.

8 Pueblo IV community house, Frijoles Canyon National Park (U.S. Soil Conservation Service, No. 114–G–NM–7130 in the National Archives, Washington, D.C.).

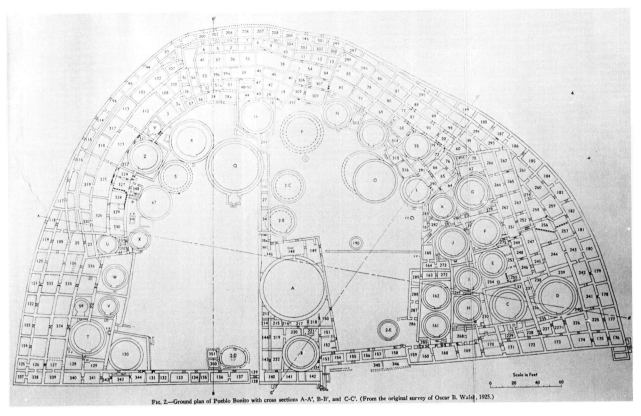

Fig. 2.—Ground plan of Pueblo Bonito with cross sections A-A', B-B', and C-C'. (From the original survey of Oscar B. Walsh, 1925.)

9   Plan of Pueblo Bonito, Chaco Canyon. The diameter of this Classic Pueblo site is more than 500 feet; the structures rose to a height of four stories. From the original survey of Oscar B. Walsh, 1925.

10   El Cerro de Chimayó, founded in 1730 but heavily restored in the early twentieth century, is the only surviving plaza-type community in New Mexico.

Learning Resources Center
Collin County Community College District
SPRING CREEK CAMPUS
Plano, Texas 75074

2

ARCHITECTURE OF THE INDIAN EPOCHS

The first permanent shelters developed in the Four Corners area were pithouses erected about A.D. 350 by Basket Maker III builders. These were subterranean or semisubterranean structures, 1 to 6 feet deep, of square or circular shape, roofed with poles covered over with earth. A characteristic of many of these was the use of four freestanding posts set in the floor to support the roof. On the tops of the posts substantial horizontal beams were placed forming a square or rectangular support for the other roof elements. Roofs of some pithouses were built flush with ground level by seating a series of horizontal poles like spokes on a wheel between the edge of the pit and the central supporting beams which were at the same height as the top of the pit. More commonly, the roof was elevated above ground level by slanting poles from the edge of the pit or from a bench circumventing the pit some distance above the floor to the central support beams which in this case were 3 to 5 feet above ground level (fig. 11). Horizontal poles were then placed between the central beams resulting in an above ground framework resembling a truncated pyramid or cone. In both cases the roof poles were covered with smaller wooden elements or brush and then with dirt or mud. A rectangular opening was left in the top of the roof to serve as a smoke hole and sometimes as an entryway. Many pithouses, however, were entered through an enclosed vestibule or passageway attached to one side of the pit. These structures ranged from 8 to 25 feet in breadth or diameter. In addition to a shallow firepit below the smoke hole and the four holes for the posts that supported the roof, there was a small ceremonial hole, the *sipapu*, which symbolized the passage from the underworld through which the Anasazi people

17

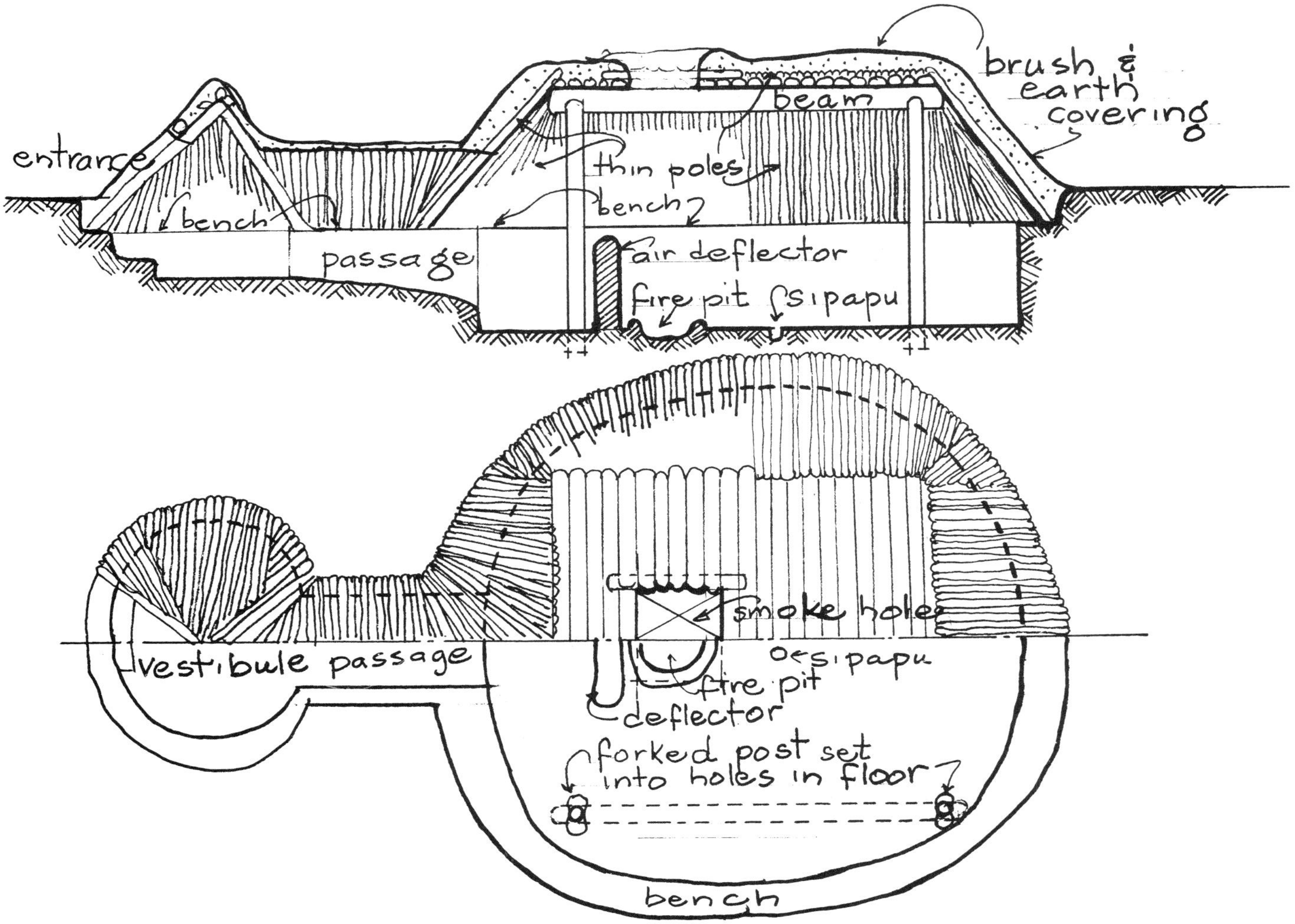

11 Hypothetical plan and section of a Basket Maker pithouse, ca. 450. Redrawn from illustration in M. H. Wormington, *Prehistoric Indians of the Southwest.*

had emerged into this world. Placed near the center of the room, the sipapu was generally 3 to 5 inches in diameter and about as deep.

The firepit was usually rimmed with stones or a collar of clay, and a low masonry wall or thin stone slab set on end formed a deflector to protect the fire in the pit from the current of fresh air that entered through the entrance vestibule. There might be several small storage pits dug in the floor, and additional storage holes might be bored in the earth walls below the shelf that supported one end of the slanting roof poles. Too high to sit on but useful for storage, this shelf is nevertheless often described by archaeologists as a bench. Excavated sites indicate that they were usually bunched together in small numbers (generally 5 to 20) in a way to suggest family groupings. In addition, there were nearby storage areas or cists excavated in the ground, covered with cone-shaped roofs of poles, and sealed inside and out with mud plaster. The small community was completed by an adjacent refuse heap.

Some changes occurred in Basket Maker III pithouses after about A.D. 450.

Most apparent was the modification of the entrance vestibule or passageway into a ventilator shaft too small for a person to crawl through. Thereafter, one entered through the smoke hole in the roof by means of a ladder. The ventilator, a right-angled shaft extending from floor level of the pithouse to the surface outside the structure, allowed fresh air to enter the house as the vestibule did in earlier times. The floor area between the ventilator opening and the firepit was portioned off from the rest of the interior by a low adobe parapet (fig. 12). Archaeologists are not agreed as to why this division exists, nor to its function. Needless to say such quarters were dark and crowded, and they were only used for household activities in inclement weather.

An important architectural innovation sometime after A.D. 700 coincided with the beginning of the Pueblo I period. For the first time rooms were constructed above ground, at first singly, then in series. The new building type is referred to as a unit, clan, or surface house. It had no windows or doors, and the rooms were entered by two ladders—one to climb to the roof, a second by which to descend into the room through the smoke hole in the roof. Wall construction was of either wattle and daub or stone laid in adobe mortar, and the flat roof was formed of contiguous poles covered with brush and adobe as were those of pithouses (fig. 13). Rooms built contiguous to one another formed an arc on the north and west sides of an irregular work area or plaza. This sequence of single-story rooms created both a wind break and a primitive line of defense,

12   Modified Basket Maker pithouse, ca. 600. Courtesy Columbia University Press.

13 Reconstruction of a Developmental Pueblo unit house and plaza. Diorama in the Museum, Mesa Verde National Park, Colorado. Courtesy Mesa Verde National Park.

though the chief means of protection was provided by the outside ladders which could be drawn up to the roof by defenders in case of attack. One interesting aspect of communities early in the period, however, is that in some cases both the new post and mud structures and the older pithouse were used simultaneously. Archaeological evidence suggests that in many such instances the pithouses served as habitations and the associated above-ground structures were used primarily as storage places. Through time, and as the surface units became more commonly employed as houses, one or more pithouses in the plaza of a village probably served as a ceremonial center for the hamlet. This ceremonial pithouse, which is the prototype of the later kiva, is clearly descended from the earlier Basket Maker pithouse. It illustrates once again in architectural history how the primitive dwelling furnished the prototype for the later religious edifice—a phenomenon repeatedly observed in different branches of world architecture.

During Pueblo II times other developments took place in Anasazi architecture. Most pueblos were constructed of stone masonry, the true kiva became a standard feature in all settlements, and the unit or clan house accreted rooms on all sides. As long as all the rooms of the group remained one story, this caused no problems since each room was lighted by means of the hatchway in the roof. But when upper stories were added, a process which probably began in Pueblo II times, ground-floor rooms deprived of light in the middle of the block were used for storage. Another characteristic of these clustered dwellings was the presence sometimes of round ceremonial chambers included in room blocks where they were encased within the rectangular grid system of walls (fig. 14). These chambers were situated at ground level instead of below grade, but like early

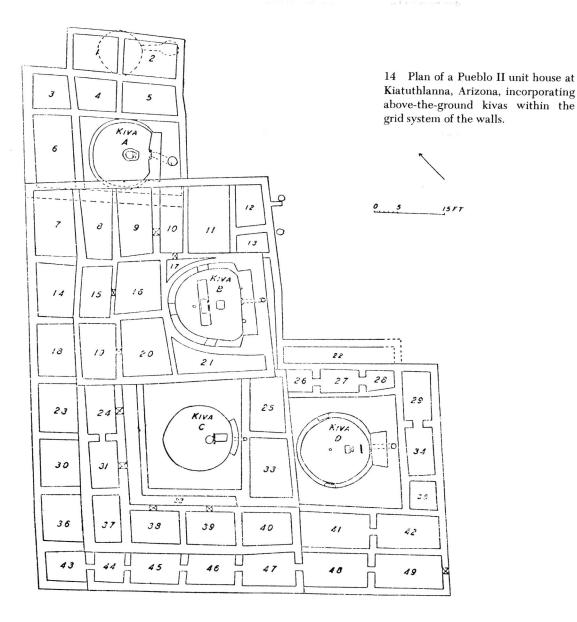

14 Plan of a Pueblo II unit house at Kiatuthlanna, Arizona, incorporating above-the-ground kivas within the grid system of the walls.

kivas, they had well-articulated ventilator shafts, were entered by ladder through the roof hatch placed above the firepit, and retained the interior bench or shelf. An interesting development here is that only certain of these chambers contained a sipapu. This suggests that not all circular rooms were employed for ceremonial purposes; some probably served social purposes—a place, for example, where male members of the clan met for weaving or for recreation.

The Pueblo III period, extending from 1050 to 1300, represents the apogee of the dominant Indian culture in the Southwest. Concentrated in the Four Corners area, it is represented by such famous sites as Chaco Canyon and Aztec Pueblo in New Mexico, Mesa Verde in Colorado, and Betatakin in Arizona. In this period the pueblos became larger in size, were fortified, and the stone masonry of which they were built attained a level of refinement unsurpassed elsewhere in southwestern Indian architecture. The size and complexity of some pueblos, the presence of regional religious centers, substantial engineering undertakings for irrigation and water storage or of highways connecting pueblos, all show a degree of community organization and control not equalled in Anasazi culture before or after.

No finer example of Pueblo III architecture exists than Pueblo Bonito, a community in Chaco Canyon, which covered three acres, contained as many as 650 rooms, and housed a population estimated at less than eleven hundred. The village was sensibly located on the north side of the canyon above the level of flooding and close enough to the canyon wall, which rose 200 feet, to find protection from winter storms. The pueblo was roughly arc-shaped (defined by a great outside wall constituted by the outer walls of the rooms, so that the overall appearance was like the letter D), constructed of stone, and over 35 feet tall. At its highest level, the structure rose to four stories. The wall is as much as 3 feet thick at ground line but thins to about one foot in the top story, has no external doors, and only small, high, slitlike window openings. From the thickness of the peripheral wall it is obvious that a multistoried structure was envisioned at the outset though the final edifice was the result of several building programs which entailed much demolition and reconstruction. Building activity largely took place between 919 and 1067. On the flat south side of the complex facing the river, protection was provided by a file of rooms only one story in height. Although there was at one time a gateway, this was blocked up and persons entering the central plaza had to cross over the roof of this line of rooms by climbing and descending ladders.

At its widest point the crescent-shaped construction is six rooms deep, and in section it steps up toward the periphery in an irregular fashion forming a series of terraces. Rooms on the ground story, even on the plaza side, had no doors but were entered by ladder through a roof hatch; upper levels, however, presumably had doors and windows opening onto the terraces. Rooms were small, averaging about 9 by 14 feet and under 8 feet in height. While rooms with outside exposures were provided with small windows, these had sometimes been blocked up, perhaps because of the cold. Such interiors cannot have been pleasant places to live, especially when one considers that smoke from any fire required for warmth or cooking found an exit as best it could through a roof hatch. It is probable that except during bad weather most household chores were carried out on the terraces or in the inner plaza; enclosed areas were primarily for storage and for sleeping during wintry seasons.

In the manner of Pueblo II unit houses, Pueblo Bonito also contained small kivas, 35 in number, some enclosed within its system of rectangular walls. Too small (the smallest is 10 feet, 4 inches in diameter) to have accommodated a large segment of the community, some of these, called clan kivas, may have been for religious purposes, others for social ends. But in either case, use was probably restricted to specific family groups or clans. Both variants retain the firepit and most have a curious alcove or shelf on the south side. It is possible that these recesses derive from the partially walled-off area found in pithouses of Basket Maker III date. Peculiar to Chaco, however, is an underfloor ventilator that connects with the usual vertical shaft. In construction these kivas depart from early pithouses by replacing the four freestanding wooden posts that supported the roof with short masonry pilasters, six to ten in number, built upon the kiva bench. These pilasters supported a roof made of log cribbing, a system that was stronger but required more and larger timbers than earlier roofs. The remains of one cribbed roof indicate that some 350 logs were required to cover an 18-foot-in-diameter kiva. Frequently the roof formed a part of a plaza or terrace in which the daily activity as well as ceremonial dances were carried on.

Besides these clan kivas, Pueblo Bonito had two chambers large enough to accommodate a goodly assembly. Called great kivas, the largest of these is 45 feet across. Its roof appears to have been supported by four heavy beams carried on four masonry piers whose placement corresponds to the four posts of a pithouse. A secondary system of logs carried the layer of earth that formed the roof. Access to these kivas was by stairs on the north-south axis rather than by ladder. The presence of two great kivas probably reflects the community's moiety organization which sought balance and reciprocity, a system of religious and social organization that survives and integrates modern pueblos.

While speaking of kivas, mention should be made of Casa Rinconada, a site in Chaco Canyon seemingly developed solely for religious activity. The great kiva, whose floor is sunk to bedrock about 5 feet below grade, has an interior diameter of 63.5 feet and its roof was supported on four piers in the manner just described (fig. 15). Access was by means of two broad stairways located north and south. No special ventilator shaft was required here because fresh air was supplied through the entrances and through numerous small windows. The stairs on the north axis communicated with a series of chambers at ground level built against the kiva's outside wall. These rooms appear to have been used for ritual and storage purposes, not for habitation. The floor of the kiva was interrupted by a large central firepit as well as by two large rectangular boxes defined by low masonry walls. These latter have been tentatively identified by archaeologists as foot drums which had skin or logs laid across the masonry rim, and upon which performers danced. They may also have been used as beds for sprouting corn or beans to be used in rituals. Two series of niches are located in the kiva wall above the level of the bench, and some people (not archaeologists) postulate that these were elements of a solar calendar that functioned in connection with the entrance opening at the head of the south stairway. This great kiva may have been built for the benefit of a number of small pueblos on the south side of the canyon or possibly for all the pueblos in the canyon.

Returning to the subject of construction, one of the most notable aspects of structures in Chaco Canyon is the stone masonry which used blocks of sandstone

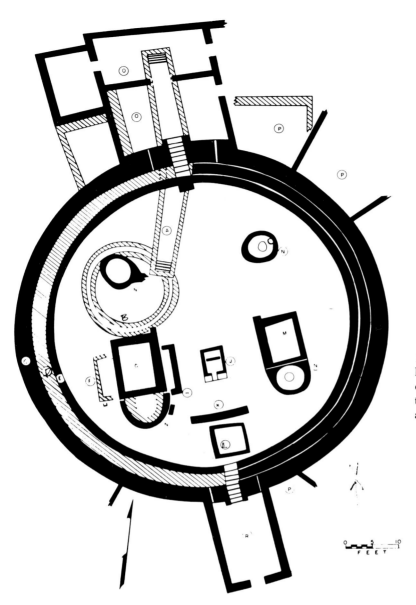

15 Plan of one of the largest community kivas (63.5 feet in diameter), Casa Rinconada, Chaco Canyon. A tree ring date places this structure tentatively between A.D. 866 and 919.

broken loose from nearby cliff walls. Some of the stone was stratified and broke easily into regular tabs. The more homogeneous material was shaped by means of stone hammers, a method of finishing that left small peck marks on the surface. An examination of several communities at Chaco Canyon provides evidence of a clear evolution of masonry technique during Pueblo III, the work becoming ever more regular and the chinking finer and more precise. Four distinct types of masonry can be distinguished, and this helps the student unravel the chronology of this complicated building. But despite the remarkably fine workmanship of this masonry, the builders did not appreciate its textural beauty: they covered it over with mud plaster. Also, despite the care with which the surface was finished, the walls were structurally weak. The actual bearing area was the rubble core

24

laid in thick mud mortar. The carefully laid faces were only a veneer. Walls were poorly bonded because the masons did not understand the advantage of an occasional course of transverse stones to act as a tie or of large stones used at corners or for jambs. More serious still, they failed to tie the many transverse walls adequately into the impressive peripheral walls that encompassed the unit. The unfortunate result is that despite the use of stone, less construction has survived than one would expect.

In spite of the arid climate, little roof timber remains at Pueblo Bonito. But the few that do provide—by examination of the tree rings' patterns—a fairly exact dating of the ruins, 919–1067. The construction of roofs was simple: one or more beams were laid across the narrow dimension of a room. These carried a system of secondary supports: a series of contiguous poles stripped of bark and placed at right angles to the beams (fig. 16). Above that a covering of reeds or bark sealed crevices between the poles so that the final 4-inch layer of earth, which formed the roof, did not silt down too badly. When a roof also served as the floor of a room above it, it is clear that the covering was completely finished before the next story was added because the ends of the secondary poles are imbedded in the masonry and the zone of masonry for the thickness of the floor is rougher than the remainder of the wall. Since a mason could not determine the exact position of the wall below after the floor covering had been completed, walls of upper stories sometimes fail to align with those below. Several original wooden ceilings are still in place in the Pueblo III ruins at Pueblo Bonito and at Aztec, New Mexico. Their preservation is due to the thick layer of rubble and earth that

16 Construction of a timber and earth roof.

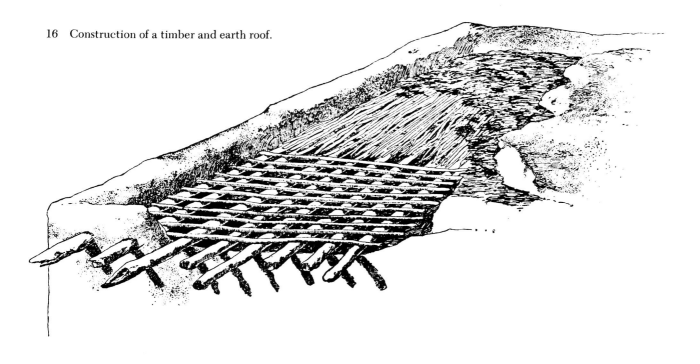

accumulated as the upper stories of the community house disintegrated and covered them.

Communication between rooms on the same level was fairly free since it was often possible to move both longitudinally and laterally, and there is evidence of vertical communication by means of interior hatchways and ladders such as those found in later Pueblo V structures. Such planning provides a minimum of privacy for the individual family and makes it difficult to guess in what way quarters were assigned or owned. Recent excavations by archaeologists indicate that some interior rooms at ground level had been filled with refuse and even used for an occasional burial before having been sealed off permanently. This would have interfered with communication between the external file of rooms which remained in use and rooms situated nearer the plaza.

Doorways usually had a raised sill (as much as one foot) and low lintel. A person entering the room therefore had to bend over considerably. Often these openings had a T-shape, and sometimes the shelves of the jamb were low enough to serve as a fulcrum on which a person could swing his feet over the sill. None of these openings had movable doors of wood. If privacy or protection against cold was desired, a skin or blanket could be hung over the opening, and there are remains of reed screens that could be rolled up. In addition to doorways, two rooms at Pueblo Bonito have corner windows which penetrate walls diagonally through corners to a room beyond, a curious and structurally unsound usage. They do, however, align with the rising sun during the winter solstice and may have been used for solar observations.

The community houses at Mesa Verde, Colorado, or Betatakin, Arizona, in better condition because of their protected location in large, shallow caves, represent a special case of Pueblo III planning. Nevertheless the presence of multistoried buildings, fine stone masonry, the interspersing of circular kivas among rectangular rooms used for dwelling, the use of kiva roofs as dance plazas or work areas, and the need for fortification renders these ruins comparable to those at Chaco Canyon and Aztec. At Mesa Verde, one finds the remains of earlier pithouses and unit houses on the mesa top above the more famous cliff houses. There, adjacent to their homes, the early inhabitants cultivated fields and constructed irrigation systems which continued to be used by the cliff dwellers; but the unsettled conditions that forced the people of Chaco Canyon to fortify their communities most likely caused the inhabitants of Mesa Verde to seek more secure sites for their villages on the protected ledges in the cliffs.

A combination of causes probably accounts for the abandonment of the northern Anasazi centers of population at the close of the Pueblo III period. Incursions of hostile forces have been hypothesized, and though none of the important ruins bear direct evidence of siege or destruction, many sites do contain sealed outside doors and windows. Inasmuch as agriculture was limited to irrigable areas, the soil might have been depleted, and there is evidence of severe erosion; or some unrecorded social or religious crisis could have prompted the people to desert their ancient haunts. One disruptive factor, a severe drought, has been dated as taking place between 1276 and 1299 by the pattern of stunted tree rings. Whatever the cause, the great pueblos were totally deserted. Probably this did not happen in one exodus since legends related by people such as the Hopi indicate that for generations their ancestors experienced a period of wandering in small groups or clans across the plains and mountains to the south of their former homes. To judge from the distinctive pottery of certain groups found at many different places, they occupied numerous intermediate sites before coming to the locations they occupied at the time the Spaniards entered the Southwest.

The positions of their new homes in the Pueblo IV period were determined by the presence of water to support agriculture: thus, they settled for 150 miles along the Rio Grande and its tributaries between Taos and Isleta, in mountainous locations in western New Mexico like Acoma and Zuñi, and on the Hopi mesas in eastern Arizona. In comparison with many Pueblo III structures in Chaco Canyon and Mesa Verde, however, most of the new communities were smaller and shoddily built. Remains of sites such as Frijoles Canyon near Los Alamos, New Mexico, or Kin-tiel near Keams Canyon, Arizona, indicate a continued need of fortification. The later builders had not forgotten how to center their living units about an internal plaza or how to protect them by stout encircling walls. On the other hand, some pueblos followed the nucleus-type unit house which had originated in Pueblo I times but was also found in Pueblo III sites like Kin Kletso at Chaco Canyon. Here dense clusters of rooms many units across piled up in irregular pyramid fashion as at Taos (fig. 17). In any event the quality of Pueblo IV stone masonry was clumsy in comparison to the exquisite work of Classical Pueblo date. Such a judgment must be qualified, however, by observing that less regular building stone was available at most new sites. At others such as Taos there was no usable stone and the Indians built with puddled adobe. Distinctly inferior to Pueblo III, Pueblo IV culture was in the process of recouping its losses when overrun by the Spanish conquistadores.

Although many ruins are known (including Bandelier, Pecos, Hawikuh, and Kuana), Taos is the only Pueblo IV community still occupied. Earlier sites in the vicinity of the present pueblo yield pottery sherds dating from the early 1300s, while portions of buildings still standing were occupied at the time of Coronado's visit in 1540. These include two large, multistoried community houses located on opposite sides of the Taos River. The northern block, which is longer than it is wide—though the width is eleven rooms—rises in irregular steps to about five stories. Because floor levels of various sections of the block are so unequal, it is difficult to specify floor levels. Originally the north block stood alone, but in recent times this isolation has been diminished by the construction of an almost continuous zone of one- and two-story rooms to the northwest.

17　Roofs of southern community house, Taos Pueblo.

As originally built, no doors or windows interrupted the walls of the ground story. For the sake of security the only entry to this "apartment house" was by ladders to the first terrace. Here interior ladders through roof hatches provided access to ground-floor rooms, the same system used earlier. From the terrace additional outside ladders gave access to upper terraces where there were small doors and slitlike windows. The factory-made doors and glass windows now in place are, of course, late nineteenth- and early twentieth-century additions. These openings illustrate a complete reversal of living habits from early times when rooms on the ground floor served mostly for storage. Fortunately, however, the new openings still are not so numerous or so large as to diminish the geometric appearance of the building with its strong sculptural and cubist character.

The small cube-shaped forms that look like dog houses and are adjacent to doors on the ground story are for wood storage. Located some distance in front of the building are freestanding *ramadas* (shelters framed of logs). Hay stored on top of the ramada also creates a shaded area where the Indians keep animals or themselves work in hot weather. Inasmuch as Taos has conservative leaders, electricity has not been brought to the main plaza, and hence there are no unsightly wires or television antennas. Anyone requiring electricity has had to erect a new house on the fringes of the pueblo. Inhabitants of the old blocks still fetch water from the Taos River, which rises in the mountains behind the pueblo, but piped water is available elsewhere in the village. Storage sheds and corrals constructed of logs, as well as outhouses, are scattered through the piñon grove to the rear of the main apartment blocks.

At the extreme northwest corner of the pueblo are the ruins of the original church. When erected in the seventeenth century, this church was situated some distance from the apartment blocks and main plaza; however, the subsequent building of new houses has linked the early church and living area. The church was damaged in 1846 during the brief revolt of Spanish and Indian forces against the United States government which had recently annexed the Territory of New Mexico. Never repaired, the old church fabric has gradually melted away so that only its outline and a stump of the tower remain; the interior of the ruined building now serves as the pueblo graveyard. The present church facing the main plaza was constructed in 1847 and drastically remodeled after World War II.

The southern unit house of Taos is somewhat triangular in outline, not so compact, and slightly lower than the north house. Kivas, seven in number, have returned to their earlier underground position on the periphery of the unit rather than being incorporated into it as at Pueblo Bonito or Kin Kletso. From an unusually detailed description written in 1776 by the Franciscan Fray Francisco Atanasio Domínguez, we know that the two blocks were then connected by a wall with towers where the wall was interrupted by the river. The same description mentions a row of rooms built at the west end of the southern block to accommodate Spanish settlers from the nearby village who had sought protection from marauding Plains Indians in the fortified pueblo. The Spaniards remained there until 1795.

Pueblo V is considered to begin about 1700, soon after the Spanish reconquest of 1693. During the twelve years the Spaniards were absent (following the Pueblo Revolt) many Indians had deserted their pueblos and migrated to high, inaccessible locations. In part they were motivated by fear of Spanish reprisals, in part by a deliberate rejection of Christianity and everything associated with the Spaniards, including many useful species of plants and animals the conquerors had introduced into the region. Reconquest was not difficult because of the inability of pueblos to cooperate in a mutual defense. Once Santa Fe had been recaptured, the Spaniards easily subdued single groups which tried to hold out against them. As each was subjugated, its members were required to return to their old home, or, if too few in number, to consolidate with another group in a new location. Reoccupied pueblos like Acoma, Zia, and Isleta were rebuilt using old foundations, while the inhabitants of Laguna, San Felipe, and other groups were settled at new, more convenient sites.

Despite their considerable age, none of these communities retains its eighteenth-century appearance because of important changes in the Indian mode of life which have encouraged repeated modification and modernization. The stabilization of nomadic tribes like the Ute, Apache, Comanche, and Navajo nullified the need for fortification. Once the Pueblos were no longer forced by fear of attack to live on the upper levels of their community houses, they began to utilize ground-floor rooms with windows and doors, or they built new blocks of unfortified houses, generally of only one story. Such a change was only sensible considering that heretofore fuel, food, and water for household needs had been carried up several levels on rickety ladders by the women and children. With disuse, the roofs and walls of unoccupied rooms on the upper levels gradually deteriorated and were finally demolished. Since most Pueblo V villages are constructed of adobe, which can easily be remodeled, openings for doors and glass windows were cut through walls as soon as the materials to make the improvements became available. The time at which this happened depended on the location of the pueblo: earlier in the Rio Grande Valley where access to Spanish and American centers was easy; not before the arrival of the railroad at places like Zuñi; and hardly before World War I in remote Hopi villages. Since World War II, however, with easy communication to all parts of the Southwest, change has everywhere accelerated. The pueblos are rapidly losing their architectural integrity as foreign materials (concrete block, aluminum windows, wrought iron porch supports, brightly painted hard stucco or even Permastone wall surfaces, hollow core doors, and ridge roofs covered with tar paper or metal sheets) disrupt the old harmony of adobe and timber that was so simple and so beautiful. The widespread introduction of fenestration employing large, undivided sheets of glass destroys the scale of the building and nullifies its solid geometric character. Similarly, the extension of house fronts to a common building line in imitation of American practice diminishes the lively modular character of the pueblo which was one of its most important visual assets. Even worse, since 1970 the federal government through HUD has instituted the construction of detached project houses on the outskirts of the pueblos. Although they do provide plumbing and central heating—elements that could also be introduced into the old clustered houses—these new government structures are constructed shoddily, made of "tickey-tackey," designed with no thought of the Pueblo tradition, and their placement on suburban type lots is ecologically unsound. In order to qualify for a low-interest government loan for their purchase, inhabitants must desert their old quarters in the heart of the pueblo to occupy the new one in the "suburbs." Thus the core of many pueblos is being depopulated, and it appears to be a matter of time until these areas will melt away as did their multistoried predecessors a century ago. (A happy exception is Tesuque which is considering rebuilding the two-story portions at its old center.) The community that best preserves the feeling and appearance of a traditional pueblo is Taos, but, as we have seen, it represents Pueblo IV, not Pueblo V design.

For a textbook example of a Pueblo V community one must turn to Zuñi as it was recorded in photographs and measured drawings about 1880. Its appearance at that time, which cannot have varied much from that of the previous century and a half, was recorded by photographer John K. Hillers and architect Victor Mindeleff. Both men were sent to Zuñi by the Bureau of American Ethnology. Hillers went there in 1879 to document Pueblo life and surroundings. Mindeleff spent the years 1880–82 in Zuñi and obtained measurements for a scale model of Zuñi to be constructed by the Bureau. (Now lost, the model was exhibited at the Columbian Exposition in Chicago and elsewhere.) The numerous views by Hillers are augmented by a few earlier (1873) photographs made by Timothy O'Sullivan, photographer for the U.S. Geological Survey West of the One Hundredth Meridian, and by later pictures (circa 1895–1910) made by Adam Clark Vroman, Ben Wittick, and Gus Nusbaum. A comparison of photographs from different dates enables the student to follow the gradual disappearance of the Pueblo V community as bit by bit it was replaced by the present one. Mindeleff and Hillers did their work in the nick of time because in 1881 the arrival of the transcontinental railroad in Gallup, New Mexico, only thirty-five miles north of Zuñi, brought the pueblo within the orbit of modern American life. From that time on the pueblo was open to increasing numbers of archaeologists, government officials, and missionaries, and the Indians were able for the first time to purchase lumber, glass, and tools with which to rebuild their community. Within a half century the blocks of multistoried houses erected in the early eighteenth century had practically disappeared except for the peripheral outlines which even today can be distinguished.

Zuñi is the sole descendant of the fabled Seven Cities of Cibola, communities purportedly built of gold, which had lured Coronado into the Southwest in 1540. The Pueblo V village was erected anew after 1705 on top of parts of the extensive Pueblo IV community known as Halona, one of the Seven Cities. The latter had been abandoned during the Pueblo Revolt when the Indians moved to the inaccessible Taaiyalanna Plateau some three miles from their old home. But whereas the old pueblo occupied both sides of the Zuñi River and was made of stone—to judge from fragments of wall that could still be seen in the late nineteenth century—the new one situated on the north bank was constructed of adobe brick.

Inasmuch as the low hill chosen as the site for the pueblo reconstruction was not high or steep enough to offer protection against armed assault, defense was provided by organizing the community around a small rectangular courtyard. Although plaza-centered, fortified communities had been common during the Pueblo III period, these usually had an elliptical or half-moon shape as at Pueblo Bonito. A rectangular deposition of banks of rooms about a plaza appears to be an innovation of Pueblo IV times, a period in which Pueblo architecture changed with unprecedented rapidity because of the frequency with which new communities were constructed as the various clans wandered in search of a permanent home.

Zuñi was not planned as a large community, and when its population grew, rooms were added wherever they could be fitted onto the existing complex, on the periphery or on top of existing rooms (fig. 18). In this way two or more stories were constructed above walls that had not been planned to support them. Rooms were even added above the two narrow streets that gave access to the plaza. Hillers' photographs show five levels of rooms though here, as at Taos, it is difficult to determine which of the many different terrace levels represents a given floor (fig. 19). At Zuñi, however, the natural rise of the hill accounts for two stories with the apartment block itself no more than three stories. Informants told Mindeleff that two generations earlier (about 1830) the main block had been two levels higher. Had that been so, the community, when viewed from the south, would have seemed seven stories in height.

When they had enveloped the original core (Blocks I and IV), the Indians began new blocks of house units, first on high ground west of the core, then down the side of the hill toward the river (Blocks II and III), and eventually on flat terrain to the southeast (Blocks VI, VII, and VIII). These later blocks were less densely grouped and lower—mostly one story (fig. 20). This diminution in density demonstrates the lessening need for defense.

The location of the church also provides some indication of how the community grew. As was generally the case with the earliest missions, the church, built in 1660, was placed on the edge of the pueblo. Damaged by fire and stripped of its roof beams during the Revolt of 1680, the church was repaired in

18 Ground plan of Zuñi Pueblo. Photograph, 1881, by Victor Mindeleff (No. 1829, in the National Anthropological Archives, Smithsonian Institution).

19 Zuñi Pueblo, looking north from Block I. Photograph, 1879, by J. K. Hillers (No. RG–106–IN–2384cy in the National Anthropological Archives, Smithsonian Institution).

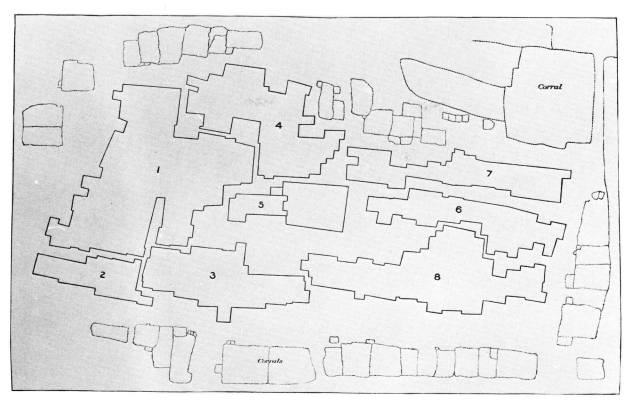

20 Zuñi Pueblo, diagram of clusters or blocks of houses, 1881.

1699 and 1705 after Spanish control was reestablished. As the community increased in size during the course of the nineteenth century, new blocks of dwellings grew up around a spacious plaza with the church in the center, a disposition quite contrary to the original plan.

An unusual aspect of Zuñi is the absence of kivas, either peripheral and below ground as at Taos or incorporated within the gridiron complex as at Pueblo Bonito. The reason for this suggested by Mindeleff was that the effective opposition mounted by the Catholic priests to native religious observances caused the Indians to move their ceremonies to rooms within the labyrinthine interior of the unit house. Although Zuñi lacks the traditional round kiva, it appears, to judge from photographs of ceremonial dances taken about 1880, that the religious center of the pueblo had remained near the original core (fig. 21).

When Hillers made his remarkable photographic record, Zuñi still retained its traditional appearance. Although some signs of change had appeared, the community was still semifortified as protection against nomadic Apache and Navajo. When troops were reduced in number in New Mexico during the Civil War, the Navajo went on a rampage which only ended in 1864 when United States forces returned to the area. Portions of the Navajo nation were then rounded up and held in captivity at Fort Sumner in eastern New Mexico until 1868. In the 1870s the Western Apache were confined to reservations in Arizona. Only then were defenses at Zuñi relaxed. This happened slowly because of the

21   Zuñi Pueblo, courtyard at core of oldest part of the pueblo. Looking northeast from Block IV. Photograph, 1879, by J. K. Hillers (No. RG–106–IN–2384–F in the National Anthropological Archives, Smithsonian Institution).

22   Zuñi Pueblo, roof terraces. Looking southwest from Block I. Photograph, 1879, by J. K. Hillers (No. 2267–i in the National Anthropological Archives, Smithsonian Institution).

conservative nature of Zuñi society and continued sporadic Apache outbreaks as late as 1886. Although the Hillers photographs show that some inhabitants had already cut doors and windows through walls of the ground story and converted to living areas room previously reserved for storage, many families still occupied the upper stories. Household activity still took place on the terraces where meats and vegetables were laid out to dry, food was cooked, children played, and old men sunned themselves (fig. 22). An essential consideration in the design of these terraces was their orientation toward the east or south. This was a functional response to the merciless sandstorms, winter winds, and blistering afternoon summer sun that came from the west. The most desirable exposure is eastern, but some southern terraces in the old multistoried core also were sheltered by the presence of a wing of rooms having a north-south axis which projected out from the west end of the main block to form a windbreak. Similarly, the higher masses of Block I sheltered low-lying Blocks VI, VII, and VIII which later grew up to the east.

While discussing terraces, mention should also be made of the thin capping stones usually laid on top of the low parapets that bounded each terrace. The purpose of these stone copings, which overhung the wall slightly and sometimes produced a crisp shadow, was to protect the adobe parapet from erosion. Similar capping stones are rare in Hopi villages of comparable date because there the walls are of crude stone masonry and because stone in thin ledges is not available. At intervals parapets were interrupted by roof drains. At first these were nothing more than a stone slab that projected beyond the face of the wall to throw off rain water, but sometimes a half log that had been hollowed was substituted, and when sawn boards became available, a boxlike drain was devised. If a drain spilled onto an adjacent roof, an inclined splash stone was laid against the wall to divert the force of the water. Probably no more than once or twice a year did enough rain fall to drain off in this fashion, since a usual rainfall was absorbed the earth blanketing the roof and was held there until it evaporated.

Another interesting aspect of Zuñi terraces was the use of many outside ladders. Mindeleff observed that they were being used in 1880 primarily for the repair of the upper stories, since few rooms above the second level were inhabited. (He also observed that some communication between rooms on different floors occupied by the same family was provided by inside ladders.) The outside ladders, which extended far above the level of the terrace, could be swung onto the roof easily and quickly in case of attack. He stated that another defense mechanism had been the removal of rungs from the holes burnt in the ladder stringers. To render these loosely put together ladders less wobbly, a wooden collar was slipped over the upper ends of the poles.

An interesting difference between Zuñi and Hopi villages, which Mindeleff studied at the same time, lies in the means of vertical access. The Hopi, living in smaller, weaker communities and being more vulnerable to Navajo raids, had not yet opened doors or windows in ground-story walls; a ladder was the only means of access to the first terrace. Above that, however, they used rough outside stairways built into the ends of walls between rooms. This use of steps instead of secondary ladders may have been caused by the scarcity of wood at Hopi. Today a similar type of outside stair can be seen in a few houses at Acoma. The presence of ovens on terraces has already been mentioned, and it might be observed that regular fireplaces for cooking were also common there. The more conservative Hopi still retained the cooking pit, a cylindrical cavity dug in the ground that functioned as a modern "fireless cooker." Such cooking pits could only be located on a terrace if a low adobe platform of sufficient (15-inch or so) depth was built up above the roof.

One of the most interesting things to look for in old pictures of Zuñi is the various types of doors and windows. By 1880 some change was already apparent, as seen in the presence of a few glass windows and doors of normal height. The use of wooden doors of any sort was in itself an innovation since prehistoric Indians did not have them. Mindeleff describes a round hole cut in a stone slab and closed with a second stone slab of rectangular or circular shape—called by the Indians a "stone close"—discovered at Kin-tiel, a Pueblo IV excavation near Keams Canyon, Arizona, as possibly typical of early portals. He also noted that the early Zuñi had a small wooden interior door made from a single log scraped down to plank size which was used to block narrow recesses in which valuables could be stored. For the most part, however, skins or blankets served to shut out cold, and if a family planned to be absent for a prolonged period, as when it left the pueblo for the summer to tend distant fields, the entrance to its apartment would simply be walled up. The Spanish introduced the pintle door—to be described in a later section—which did not require metal hinges, but boards and squared timber were necessary to make them. The Indians did not have these items until the Spanish introduced metal tools. Even when they got these, according to Mindeleff, they used small knives to shape the mortise and tenons for their joinery. Sometimes the rail and stiles were bound together with rawhide.

A few American mill-sawn boards may have been available after the late 1860s when Fort Wingate was rebuilt on a more permanent scale, but Mindeleff noted that as late as 1881 a sawn board at Zuñi was a highly prized possession. The pre-American pintle doors were very low (3½ to 4 feet) and placed on a high (12-inch) sill. In early photographs, the squat proportions of these doors disguise the low ceiling heights and make the Zuñi apartment house appear larger than it really was. The occasional use of a regulation (6 foot, 8 inch) door, which must have been a recent addition when the picture was made, reveals the building's true size (fig. 23).

Great variation in fenestration was also evident. Windows ranged from openings that could not be closed to those filled with wood grills, selenite, or glass. Window openings varied from small (4-inch) to large holes whose

23 Zuñi Pueblo, Block I, looking northwest from the church. Photograph, 1911, by Gus Nussbaum (No. 2303–A–1 in the National Anthropological Archives, Smithsonian Institution).

placement varied from floor level to just under the roof. To close them one stuffed in rags or walled them up with adobe. Some openings were filled with a slab of selenite, a translucent gypsum material mined in the area. Available in sizes up to 10 x 18 inches, most pieces were smaller; often a panel was pieced together of fragments and then "cemented" with mud plaster (fig. 24). These panels, set on a slight angle, were supported inside by short wooden sticks. The Spaniards probably introduced the use of selenite as no traces of it used for fenestration have been found in Pueblo IV ruins. Furthermore, it would have been difficult to cut without metal tools. Unknown before the Americans arrived,

24 Zuñi Pueblo, a selenite window, 1881.

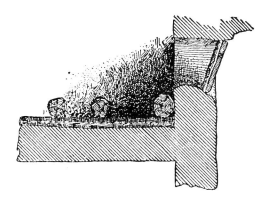
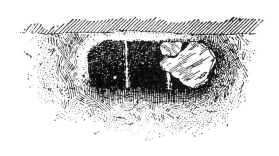

window glass was present at Zuñi in small amounts by 1879, and was either embedded in the masonry (like selenite slabs) or set in fixed wooden sash. Mindeleff comments on the disparity of technological levels then employed at Zuñi which, despite the strong communal nature of the society, varied greatly with the wealth of the builder. Poor inhabitants built in the manner of earlier generations; the wealthy employed "up-to-date" American techniques.

Of particular interest is the presence of door and window openings cut through the roof. The traditional method of entering a room since Pueblo I times had been through a roof hole that also served as the smoke hole. The perimeter of the hatchway was usually built up with a rim of stone to prevent rain water from

25 Zuñi Pueblo, an oblique window, 1881.

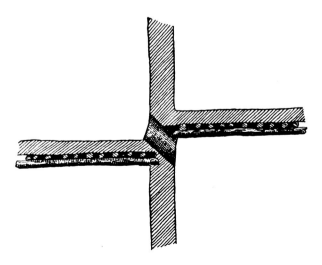

draining into the interior. A light hole was similar in construction but smaller, and often a cover made from a thin stone slab was provided. In such instances the profile of the stone rim was inclined so as to throw off rain. An additional type of fenestration is the oblique window, a kind of clerestory that opened above the level of the terrace but entered the adjacent room of the story below just under its ceiling. In section, therefore, it formed a diagonal tunnel (fig. 25). Its obvious disadvantages, of course, were the small amounts of light and air that it could provide and the danger of draining roof water into the room, but it could easily be blocked with a stone. Oblique and roof windows were much more numerous at Zuñi than in any Hopi community studied by Mindeleff. The reason for this was the organic, additive growth of Zuñi over the years. As room-cells were added to the nucleus, thus blocking outside windows, the only remaining source of light was through openings in the roof. When a new room was constructed on top of an old one already surrounded by others, the only means of obtaining light was through the curious oblique window.

One other architectural feature of prominence at Zuñi is the chimney. Beginning as nothing more than a smoke hole situated above one corner of a room and protected by a rim of stone or adobe, the chimney was gradually heightened to improve the draft. Sometimes constructed of stone or adobe, it had both circular and square cross sections, but often the chimney was composed of a stack of clay pots whose bottoms had burned out (fig. 26). The pots might be exposed or plastered over. If a chimney had to rise a full story above a roof; the easiest place to build a chimney was a re-entrant corner.

Room interiors at Zuñi were small and simple but aesthetically pleasing. Sizes of ordinary rooms varied from 7 x 9½ to 9 x 11 feet; ceiling heights were 6 to 8 feet. The roof was supported with the usual system of beams and cross poles covered by a layer of earth. Since spans were not great, beams of between 6 to 8 inches in diameter placed at approximately three-foot intervals were adequate; much smaller members, with diameters between 1½ to 2 inches, were sufficient for the cross poles. As in prehistoric construction, these ceilings were sealed with reeds or brush, then plastered with adobe, packed with several inches of earth, and coated again with mud. Occasionally at Zuñi a room was paved with flagstones, even on an upper level. Walls plastered with mud were often divided into two zones, an upper one of light color and a darker dado. Rooms with mural decorations also occurred but they may have been used for ceremonial purposes. As there were a minimum number of openings, the geometric content of these interior spaces was clearly stated. Sculptural variation was provided by occasional wall niches of varied shapes and placement, some of them formed when windows had been walled up. A hanging pole for blankets or ritual paraphernalia ran the width of the room near one wall or was placed diagonally in a corner.

Some rooms might contain an adobe *banco* (bench) against one or more

26　Zuñi Pueblo, looking west from roof terraces of Block I. Photograph, 1879, by J. K. Hillers (No. RG–106–IN–2384cw, in the National Anthropological Archives, Smithsonian Institution).

walls, but movable furniture was practically unknown (fig. 27). People sat and slept on rugs on the floor, stowed possessions on shelves in niches, and stored food in masonry bins built against a wall. The most prominent piece of internal "furniture" was a mealing bin, a stone-lined trough divided into compartments in which corn was ground. The bin was placed near a corner but sufficiently far from the wall so that women, facing into the room, could kneel to grind meal (fig. 28). Using stone manos and metates, the grinding was carried out in three steps (coarse, medium, and fine) with a fourth bin sometimes present for storage.

The large variety of fireplace designs present at Zuñi demonstrates that in 1880 builders there were still experimenting with this architectural form only recently (after the Revolt) borrowed from the Spanish. Originally, of course, the fire had been built in a shallow firepit in the center of the room. The first step toward a fireplace, as already noted, was a move to one corner, above which a smoke hole was cut. Evidence for such an arrangement was provided by smoked walls in some rooms. The addition of a hood to catch the smoke and direct it toward the hole was the next improvement. Although a number of solutions evolved for the support of this hood, its construction was always light: it was often made of thin poles, cane, or even sunflower stalks coated on both surfaces with mud plaster. These flimsy and highly flammable covers survived only because fires burned on the hearth were small due to the shortage of fuel. Beams supporting these corner hoods were ingeniously arranged involving a single pole cantilevered from one wall carrying both the second pole and the hood, poles cantilevered from both walls, or a bent pole whose ends were embedded in both walls (fig. 29). Sometimes the intersecting lintels were supported on a forked upright stick or suspended by a rawhide thong from the ceiling. Since stone in thin layers was available at Zuñi, slabs of that material were also used for lintels cantilevered from the wall or for the upright support (fig. 30). In a more complicated arrangement, which had a mantel and was copied from Spanish examples, one side of the "corner" fireplace was placed against a spur buttress thrown out from a wall for the purpose. If the hearth in any of these designs was raised at all, it was hardly more than six inches. Fireplaces of comparable design were also built outside on terraces where most of the cooking was done.

It is interesting that the nearest thing to a hearth possessed by Pueblo IV Indians had been the piki oven, a long (up to 24 inches), narrow stone grill supported on low (12-inch), parallel adobe walls (fig. 31). The stone slab, treated with resin to prevent cracking and heated by means of a low fire, was used to cook a ceremonial cornbread called piki wafers. Though bearing a superficial resemblance to later iron stoves with long, flat tops, these ovens did not permit a draft to pass through them since only one end was open, and they were not connected with a flue. Mindeleff observed some piki ovens alongside a hearth below a single smoke hood. He also noted examples of adobe "andirons" on the hearth, as well as of ingenious "burners," the adobe supports of which conformed

27 Zuñi Pueblo, interior with fireplace and bancos. Photograph attributed to A. C. Vroman, ca. 1900 (No. 2297, in the National Anthropological Archives, Smithsonian Institution).

to the rounded bottom of a pot with space left between the supports for a small fire.

Of dwellings standing in Zuñi in 1880, virtually no trace remains today except for the general outline of the several island-like blocks of buildings. One by one they disappeared because of neglect or structural failure. The walls of many ground-floor rooms constructed to support no more than a roof were inadequate for the one or more stories imposed on them as the pueblo grew. Mindeleff mentions the collapse of a tier of rooms on the west side of the original courtyard a year after he had measured the complex. Rooms on the upper stories not kept in repair after they ceased to be used melted away so that by 1911 only a shell of one room on the topmost level remained. Rooms in use at ground level, on the other hand, were replaced by larger ones with higher ceilings and modern doors and windows. But as larger, more regular units of composition were substituted for old ones of smaller size and varied elevation, the splendid scale of

28 Zuñi Pueblo, a mealing bin. Photograph attributed to A. C. Vroman, ca. 1900 (No. 2259 in the National Anthropological Archives, Smithsonian Institution).

the old community was lost. Because of its organic growth in conformity with a given set of requirements, the old edifice had possessed infinite variety tempered by a fine sense of order. The key to this order was the way in which all walls conformed to coordinate axes. Despite the extent of the complex, each house with its terrace was unique, and even though many persons lived in proximity, a sense of individuality and distinctiveness was preserved. This was an achievement from which modern urban designers could learn much.

The process of the disintegration and rebuilding of Zuñi can be followed in a series of photographs made between 1873 and 1911 (figs. 32–34). In early pictures a series of rooms extends for about 50 feet along the top story, while below, the occasional new room of normal size reveals by contrast the smallness of the old construction. The greater size and number of later glass windows, though undoubtedly making for more pleasant interior living spaces, diminish the strong geometric effect of the massing and destroy the earlier harmonious scale. The

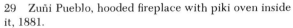
29 Zuñi Pueblo, hooded fireplace with piki oven inside it, 1881.

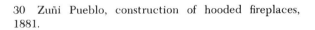
30 Zuñi Pueblo, construction of hooded fireplaces, 1881.

31 Shumopavi (Hopi) Pueblo, Arizona, hooded fireplace, piki stone, and primitive andiron, 1881.

32 Zuñi Pueblo, Block I, looking northwest from the church. Photograph, 1873, by T. H. O'Sullivan (No. 34,068–D in the National Anthropological Archives, Smithsonian Institution).

declining use made of the terrace is also documented in the slow disappearance of the loggia on the third terrace which still had its roof in the 1873 picture. According to Mindeleff, the third terrace, in Hopi called the "utpa'tea," was used for social purposes (visiting, congregating, sitting in the sun) and was considered communal property. One thing about the process of renewal that may be difficult to understand from pictures is the way rooms on lower levels appear to be reconstructed entirely, while those above them remain unchanged. It should be borne in mind, however, that the village stood on a slope, and the rooms undergoing repair on the lowest stories were in fact located in front of the multistoried block.

A good deal of fine ashlar masonry was done at Zuñi between World Wars I and II. The use of large, well-shaped stones appears to have been introduced by government people as well as by Mormon missionaries who moved into the area. By 1880, anthropologist Frank Cushing, who was sponsored by the Bureau of American Ethnology, had erected a stone house on the south side of the Zuñi River. Stone was employed later for several business blocks and public buildings in Gallup, New Mexico. In this vein, substantial tribal and private edifices were

33 Zuñi Pueblo, Block I, looking northwest from the church. Photograph, ca. 1885, by Ben Wittick (No. 41,831–B in the National Anthropological Archives, Smithsonian Institution).

34 Zuñi Pueblo, Block I, looking northwest from the church. Photograph, 1899, by A. C. Vroman (No. 2293–B in the National Anthropological Archives, Smithsonian Institution).

erected at Zuñi between 1910 and 1930. Since World War II, however, this handsome material has given way to concrete block and still more recently to "tickey-tackey" camouflaged with cement plaster.

In this manner the Pueblo V village of Zuñi has virtually disappeared, though a few walls or even whole rooms may still be hidden in the heart of one of the blocks. Since World War II, however, the tendency has been not to rebuild on the original family plot within the core of one of the blocks, but to leave the old home to disintegrate while constructing a detached dwelling on the periphery of the community. In this way the early core composed of dense clusters of rooms has been reduced to scattered dwellings separated by empty spaces and passageways where none had existed. The ground level has also risen where tiers of adobe walls collapsed. Despite these changes the outline of the early blocks can still to a large extent, be distinguished. This is demonstrated by a comparison of Mindeleff's careful ground plan of 1881 and a photogrammetric survey carried out by Perry Borchers in 1973 (fig. 35).

As the core was deserted, new construction was located at first along the old road, now Highway 53, that runs along the north side of the pueblo. In a sense this has become Main Street, especially since the erection of an extensive tribal building for offices and community center. A second street traversing the river and extending south has also become a focus of development with a school, two

35   Zuñi Pueblo, photogrammetric record, 1973, by Perry Borchers.

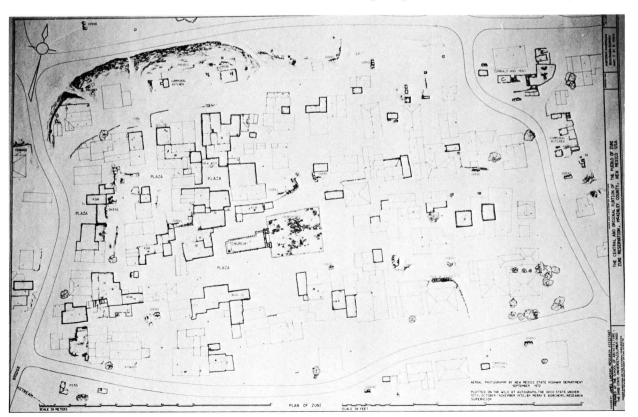

trading posts, and numerous dwellings. In this southern zone no traces of Pueblo IV Halona are now visible, although excavations in 1888 revealed foundations. A serious effacement involved the construction in 1972 of a paved boulevard encircling the old pueblo and cutting it off from the river toward which it had always been oriented. About a mile to the southwest stands the new government-subsidized suburb containing two- and three-bedroom stuccoed houses with aluminum windows, half-acre lots, and paved streets. Resembling cheap tract developments anywhere in America, but here set in a treeless desert where the sand blows and every drop of water is precious, these constructions, which were supposed to improve the living conditions of the rural poor, are as aesthetically sterile and ecologically unsound as any that could have been devised. Developments identical to this, alas, are found in almost every pueblo in the region.

3

SPANISH COLONIAL BUILDING

Although Francisco Vásquez de Coronado led an exploratory expedition into New Mexico as early as 1540, no officially sanctioned permanent Spanish settlement was attempted until 1598 when don Juan de Oñate settled San Gabriel, near present San Juan Pueblo. San Gabriel was abandoned, however, and the community moved to Santa Fe, which was to become the Spanish administrative center for the province, in 1610. The first Franciscans arrived in the 1580s and began the enormous task of Christianizing the indigenous population.

Throughout the colonial period, the Spanish population remained small in comparison with the Indian population. In 1650 there were approximately 1,000 Spaniards and 25,000 Indians. After the Reconquest there were about 2,000 Spaniards. Fray Francisco Atanasio Domínguez, the Franciscan inspector who visited New Mexico in 1776 to report on the conditions of the missions, recorded a total of 18,261 souls—about 8,000 Pueblo Indians, and 10,261 Spaniards—in communities where friars were active. (This figure did not include the El Paso district, or some of the peripheral Spanish settlements.) By the end of the colonial period, estimates placed the number of Spaniards at 25,000; the number of Indians at 17,000.

During the eighteenth century, the Spanish population greatly increased. This can be attributed to the immigration of destitute Spaniards and mestizos from economically depressed mining towns in northern Mexico, and also to the decision of land-hungry soldiers who, upon discharge from the Santa Fe garrison, took up residence on grants of land at the periphery of Spanish settlement. At this time the Spanish population of New Mexico was made up of a few crown officials, a handful of merchants and wealthy landowners, a proportionately large number of laborers (both Spanish and mestizo) who worked either on the larger land grants or on small plots of their own, and friars assigned to Indian mission and Spanish communities. For the crown-appointed governor and his staff, New Mexico must have been a kind of Siberia; their major concern was to wring such wealth as they could from the province before returning to Mexico. People living on community land grants were torn between the need to live in isolated—and more than a little dangerous—areas if they wished to maintain their grants, and their fear of Indian raids. Spaniards, settlers and friars alike, who lived outside of Santa Fe had to see to their own well-being since the military could not assure them constant protection. The Santa Fe presidio was hardly formidable: throughout the eighteenth century it seldom had more than 120 soldiers. Thus, protection, and often punitive expeditions against hostile nomadic Indians, came from the colonists themselves and their Pueblo Indian auxiliaries.

The first Spaniards had come to New Mexico with expectations of great wealth. It did not take them long to discover that the economic possibilities of the area were extremely limited. The economy of the Rio Grande area in pre-Spanish times had been based primarily on agriculture, although evidence increasingly points to the fact that trade between Mexican and New Mexican Indians was carried on to some extent. Despite Spanish contributions in the form of metal tools and many species of domestic animals and plants, the area's economy remained one of bare subsistence. Even the large landowners had few material possessions besides acreage and livestock: what differentiated them from the poor was the power they wielded over their Spanish and Indian laborers. Wills of some of the wealthier landowners reveal their scarcity of material wealth. On the whole, there appears to have been little difference between the standards of living of the Spanish and Indian populations. The Spaniards, for example, often fought and hunted with bows and arrows. In fact, in 1846, some soldiers recruited to fight American forces were still using bows and arrows.

New Mexico was far enough removed from the markets of Mexico to make trade between the two centers difficult and expensive. The fifteen-hundred-mile trek from Mexico City to Santa Fe required six months of travel. That and the hazards of the route—caused by harsh terrain and hostile Indians—augmented the price of goods so that even insignificant articles became too expensive for the average New Mexican. During the early colonial period, the only source of imported goods was the missionary supply service financed by the Spanish crown. New Mexico offered Indian blankets, crudely woven cloth (*jerga*), salt, animal hides, and piñon nuts in trade. Coinage was practically nonexistent since people relied almost entirely on barter for their business transactions.

By the early nineteenth century, feeble attempts were made to trade with Mexico and a few enterprising merchants were sending caravans to the Chihuahua January Trade Fair. Several ranchers drove herds of cattle or sheep to San Juan de los Lagos in Jalisco. In 1850, the Luna and Otero families, demonstrating unusual enterprise, drove 25,000 cattle from the Rio Grande Valley to the gold mining district of California. All such activity was small-scale and sporadic. By the 1870s, it was California ranchers who were shipping superior breeds of livestock east to sell in New Mexico. Throughout both the Spanish and Mexican periods economic existence of the province was to remain precarious.

Given so narrow a margin of existence, it is not surprising that there was little technological or cultural innovation. There was little energy and less capital for developing fields which would have resulted in immediate economic benefit to the colony. For example, silver, which existed in substantial deposits, was not exploited until the 1880s. Although good clay abounded, and Spaniards in Mexico were conversant with brick- and tile-making, in New Mexico the industry was unknown. Moreover, despite ample water power and excellent stands of timber in the mountains of New Mexico, the colonists did not devise a water-driven sawmill. Throughout the colonial and Mexican periods, the level of technology did not essentially change.

One deterrent to economic growth during the colonial period was depredations by Indians. First the Apaches, then the Comanches and Utes, and later the Navajos, harassed Spaniards and Pueblo Indians alike. After acquiring the horse, which had been unknown in America before the coming of the Spaniards, the way of life of these indigenous people altered greatly; they became highly mobile, and in times of scarcity they found it easy to cross the mountains, sweep down upon a settlement, and carry off what they needed. The Indian threat was so serious that Spanish settlers in the Taos Valley, for example, deserted their own village in 1776 for quarters within the walls of Taos Pueblo. Fray Francisco Atanasio Domínguez describes this arrangement in detail and comments on the seriousness of the nomadic incursions. Because of this the Spaniards long remained bottled up in the valleys of the Rio Grande and its tributaries. It was to divert surprise attacks or to take the brunt of them that community land grants like those of Las Trampas (1751), Abiquiu (1744), and Ojo Caliente (1764) were given to groups of impoverished families who would agree to reside on them.

Social customs and even the language remained remarkably conservative. As late as the twentieth century, linguists discovered New Mexicans employing words and expressions from the seventeenth century which had long since passed out of usage in Spain and Mexico. Architecture demonstrates the same phenomenon: forms and methods of building introduced about 1610 were still in use more than two centuries later.

With the exception of the much remodeled Palace of the Governors in Santa Fe, significant remains of seventeenth- and eighteenth-century Spanish architecture in New Mexico are confined to a handful of mission churches. These consist of five buildings from the seventeenth century (damaged in the Revolt but repaired and still in use), five more in ruins but of architectural significance, twelve churches of eighteenth-century origin (seven have been drastically altered), and seven more from the nineteenth century which today retain enough of the early tradition to be studied profitably. Less is known about the homes in which the Spanish colonists lived than about Indian dwellings of the previous thousand years.

Mission work in the Province of New Mexico was entrusted to the Franciscan order, and their activity here constitutes an extension of the pioneering work which they began three generations earlier (after 1523) in Mexico. In New Mexico the missionaries were confronted by many of the same problems they had faced in Mexico, and they used many of the same solutions. In both places the ratio of natives to friars was overwhelming. In the beginning exotic languages had to be mastered before conversion could begin, though by the seventeenth century the Indians were more and more being forced to learn Castilian. Great distances between isolated pueblos forced the friars to be self-reliant. In neither area could a friar depend on arms to force conversion or construction of a mission station; in such endeavors he had only his own good example and his powers of persuasion. In both areas, also, the Franciscans sought to protect the natives from the Spanish administrators and civilians who continually attempted to exploit them. As a result tension soon developed between the friars and the rest of the Spanish population.

The friar was also on his own in matters of church construction. Lacking professional advice or any kind of training, except for what he learned on the job, the friar had to be designer, engineer, job captain, and building inspector. Thus, he fell back on the experience the order had gained in Mexico and repeated the basic mission station design in use there. In popular terms we may refer to this as a "fortress church," a definition that is visually descriptive if historically inaccurate inasmuch as these structures were neither designed nor used for defense purposes. Differences between Mexican and New Mexican building programs were that stations in New Mexico were smaller, of simpler construction (i.e., without vaulted ceilings), and built of adobe rather than stone. (This comparison is between the earlier and more elaborate mission stations in the valleys of central Mexico where the population was dense and the pre-Conquest standard of building high. In remote parts of Mexico, especially in the north, stations were simpler and more comparable to those along the Rio Grande.)

Several conditions required such simplifications in New Mexico. The small population of Pueblo Indians, in contrast to that of the Aztecs or Mixtecas, had never developed a special class of builders with a high level of building technology. They had no tradition of stone building, at least of any that involved shaping or carving stone, and masonry was done by the women. Men traditionally worked only with wood: felling trees, carrying them down from the forests, shaping and lifting them into place. At the very outset in New Mexico the friars decided against teaching the Indians methods of European stone construction or developing a special class of masons. The one significant thing they did do in this area was teach the Indians to shape mud into bricks.

Basically the mission station consisted of two parts: the church and living quarters for the missionary (referred to as a *convento*). The church was the more important: tall and approximately four times as long as it was wide, it dominated the low-lying adjacent convento (fig. 36). In New Mexico the nave (with the exception of that at Pecos) was never wider than 33 feet and the height was slightly greater than the width. (In Mexico the nave was frequently 35 feet wide and 70 feet high.) Chapels or transepts, which might contain side altars, were absent, and the apse was narrower than the nave in order to focus attention on the high altar (fig. 37). This spatial simplification appears to have been a conscious attempt to demonstrate in visual terms the monotheistic nature of Christianity as opposed to the polytheistic religions of the Aztec or Pueblo Indians. Over the main entrance was a loft used for the choir.

The space of the nave was made as large and as high as possible. Inasmuch as the Indians (Aztec as well as Pueblo) had previously experienced no large, clear spaces that were enclosed, they seem to have been duly impressed by these ample church interiors and thus by the cult for which they had been erected.

36 Hypothetical plan and section of a New Mexico mission church.

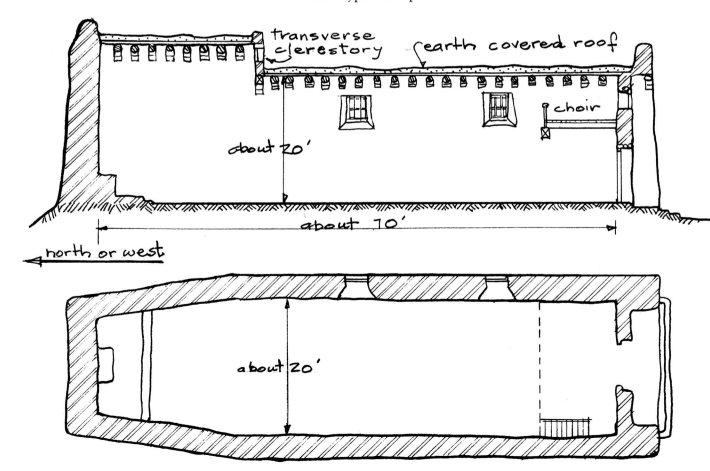

37   Isleta Pueblo, interior of San Agustín church, built by 1629 and restored in 1695.
Photograph, 1938.

Fenestration in New Mexico churches was limited to two or three small windows plus a transverse clerestory opening located just in front of the altar. This overhead opening introduced a flood of light into the otherwise somber interior and dramatically illuminated the high altar. In order for the clerestory to take advantage of the sunrise, at which time the population was expected to attend mass, New Mexican churches were oriented with the apse to the west or north. The only bit of architectural embellishment of the New Mexican interior was provided by corbels which supported the roof beams. The plain wall behind the altar was probably decorated with paintings done on buffalo hides or with a simple mural painted in earth colors directly on the adobe plaster.

Although these churches lack decoration, they possess a striking massiveness that imparts a fine sculptural quality. As in the fortress churches of Mexico, the façades inevitably contain a large double door above which is a single window that lights the choir loft. Some variation in façade composition exists in New Mexico: there are churches with twin towers, with only one tower, with a low projecting vestibule, with a balcony between heavy end buttresses, or with an *espadaña*. Early photographs indicate that walls were originally capped by crenals as in Mexico. Another similarity was the presence of a walled atrium with a cross located in its center, directly on axis with the entrance.

Contiguous with the church and generally located on its south side (to gain protection from winter winds) was the *convento*. Here a single file of rooms laid around a patio provided ample space for the single friar and his staff of six or seven Indian retainers. Here also tithes were stored. Often a second patio and/or corral were attached to the rear of the convent. Occasionally, as at Acoma and Laguna, the convento included rooms on the second story, thereby more nearly resembling mendicant establishments in Mexico.

An interesting exception to the standard construction just described is provided by three stations in the Manzano Mountains (at Abó, Quarai, and Humanas pueblos) and by one at Giusewa Pueblo in the Jémez Mountains. As good ledge stone is available in each of these communities, that material was employed instead of adobe brick for the church as well as for the nearby Indian village. These missions, thus, are relatively well preserved despite the fact that all have been abandoned since the seventeenth century. The three churches in the Manzano range, in contrast to the more usual single-aisle plan, contained transepts.

In addition to these stone ruins, five adobe pre-Rebellion churches are preserved: Zia, 1614; Isleta, 1629; Acoma, by 1644; Halona (Zuñi), circa 1660; El Paso (Ciudad Juárez), 1662. Following the Reconquest of New Mexico, they were repaired and have been in use more or less ever since. (Halona, repaired in 1704, was abandoned a second time before 1846 and restored again by the National Park Service in 1966.) These churches demonstrate that architectural solutions introduced into the area at the outset of Spanish dominion continued to be used for more than 200 years, as long as Spanish culture dominated the region.

Modifications in church design in the course of the eighteenth century were minor. Spanish communities usually employed a cruciform plan (Santa Cruz, 1733; Las Trampas, 1761; Ranchos de Taos, circa 1780; Albuquerque, circa 1790) while churches in pueblos followed the single-aisle scheme (Laguna, circa 1700; Cochiti, circa 1720; Picurís, circa 1780). Undoubtedly the Spanish preference for a cruciform arrangement was a response to the characteristic solution long before adopted in Spain and Mexico for parish churches, but the vaults and domed crossing employed there were beyond the technical capacities of New Mexican builders. When using the cross plan, the traditional transverse clerestory window was moved forward so as to illuminate transepts and crossing as well as the apse. Churches erected in Spanish communities lacked the attached convento for a practical reason: they had no friar since they were not missions supported by a crown subsidy. Some Spanish communities like Las Trampas or Ranchos de Taos were classed as *vistas;* that is, they received periodic visits from the priest assigned to a nearby pueblo mission. In such instances a single room might be attached to the sacristy where the priest could stay overnight when occasion demanded. Larger Spanish communities such as Santa Fe, Santa Cruz, or Albuquerque were able to support a resident friar, but he lived in a rectory separate from the church. Except for such minor adjustments, buildings of the later eighteenth century are almost indistinguishable from earlier ones.

Even the nineteenth century added nothing new to the basic church building. This is demonstrated by structures in both Spanish communities (Chimayó, 1816; Talpa, 1840; or El Valle, 1870) and Indian pueblos (Taos, 1849; Santo Domingo, 1890; Santa Clara, 1918). Chimayó especially demonstrates the continuity that existed here because it is so well preserved (fig. 38). Indeed the conservative tradition survived in New Mexico long enough to merge with a conscious revival before World War I of Spanish colonial forms.

In addition to ecclesiastical, there was, of course, a good deal of domestic building. Although the popular conception of a "typical" Spanish colonial dwelling is that of a house built around a central patio, such houses were not common. Excavations to the east of Albuquerque underway in 1975–76 have uncovered the remains of a frontier hamlet sometimes referred to as Carnué. Occupied briefly in the 1760s but abandoned because of Indian depredations, it reveals the stark simplicity of dwellings occupied by some Spaniards. Most of the houses consist of a single room plus an attached shelter that was probably covered with corn stalks and hay. They generally had a corner fireplace and an outside *horno*, a beehive oven of adobe similar to those found in Mediterranean countries. The houses were grouped irregularly around two plazas, and there is evidence of a crude (and presumably hastily constructed) defense wall of adobe

38 El Santuario, Chimayó, 1816. The church plan changed little during two centuries. Photograph, 1934.

surrounding the community (fig. 39). The typical house of the seventeenth century probably consisted of two or three rooms. As the late E. Boyd observed, the Spaniards preferred a few multipurpose rooms that were relatively large to the numerous small rooms used by Indians. Few families were wealthy enough to afford large homes in the first instance, although some succeeded in obtaining a grant of land and building a seigniorial residence. An extensive dwelling apportioned among several heirs soon lost its visual unity as some owners neglected their rooms when they quarreled with relatives or moved away. It is not uncommon to find a once-large establishment in various stages of disrepair as separate owners remodeled, maintained, or neglected their particular rooms without regard for the unified appearance of the building.

Such a large residence is, nevertheless, a good type with which to begin our discussion. A typical hacienda, or house, was rectangular, perhaps as large as 100 x 175 feet, and built around two courtyards, one in front called a *placita* or *plazuela,* and one in the back that served as a corral (fig. 40). The whole complex was closed within high adobe walls which, until the mid-nineteenth century, had no windows or doors, only two sets of gates. The front gate opened to a *zaguán,* a covered passage wide enough to permit a wagon to pass to the placita. The rear gate opened into the corral.

The placita contained a well and was encircled by a series of rooms arranged in single file. These rooms, perhaps twelve or fourteen in number and of differing sizes, housed the various household activities. A narrow passage connected the placita with the corral. Barns, storerooms, sheds for cattle and poultry, and probably a privy, were found in the corral. One house which survived until the

60

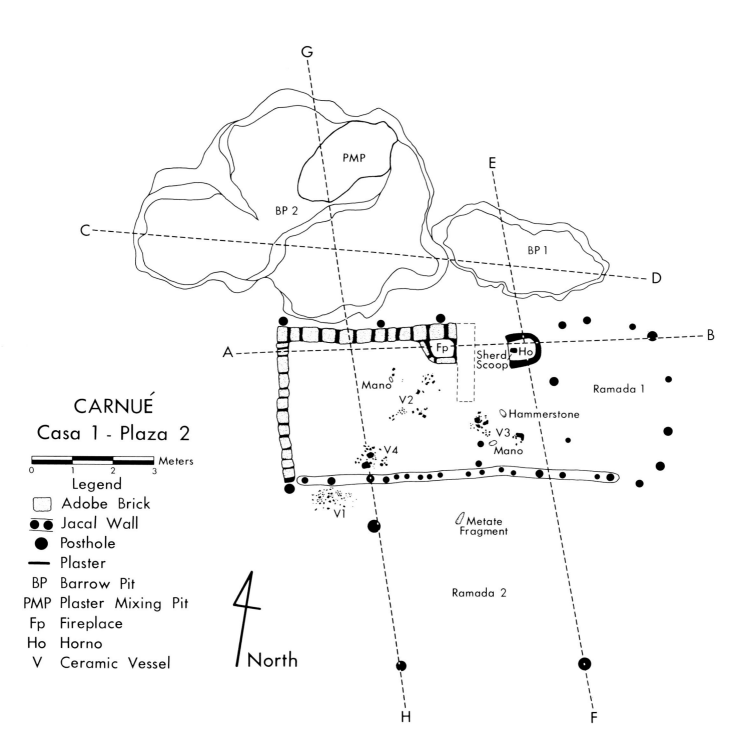

CARNUÉ
Casa 1 - Plaza 2

Meters
0   1   2   3

Legend
Adobe Brick
Jacal Wall
Posthole
Plaster
BP   Barrow Pit
PMP Plaster Mixing Pit
Fp   Fireplace
Ho   Horno
V   Ceramic Vessel

North

PMP

BP 2

BP 1

Fp

Sherd Scoop   Ho

Mano

V2

Hammerstone

V3

Mano

V4

Ramada 1

Metate Fragment

V1

Ramada 2

A   B   C   D   E   F   G   H

39   Plan of a one-room house in Carnué, 1760s. Two of the walls are of thin adobe masonry;
at least one is jacal; the construction of the fourth is uncertain.

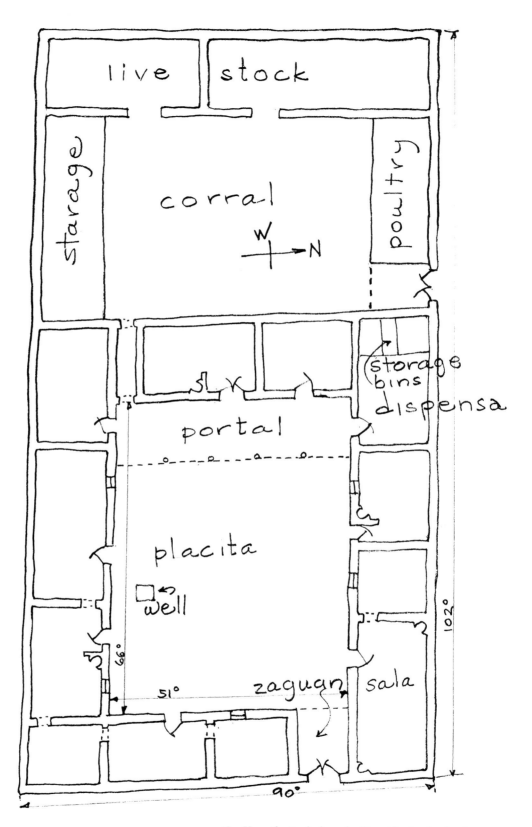

live stock

storage

corral

W → N

poultry

storage bins
dispensa

portal

placita

well

zaguan

sala

66°

51°

102°

90°

40 Hypothetical plan of a New Mexico hacienda.

1950s, also contained a ramp leading to the roof where various foodstuffs were laid out to dry and where once there had been a smokehouse. A smaller hacienda might lack the attached corral if served by outlying barns and sheds constructed of wood, or rooms might extend around only two or three sides of the placita with a strong curtain wall and gate to complete the enceinte.

In an era when Indian incursions were common, such houses, without outside windows and few doors, were fortresses in a very real sense. The gates were strong and the placita and corral large enough to contain the family's horses and cattle in case of emergency. One of the few surviving haciendas, the Antonio Severino Martínez house near Taos, built by 1827, was equipped with a parapet provided with loopholes above the roof level from which defenders might fight off Indian attackers.

The differences between a hacienda and a modest dwelling were actually minimal. Each consisted of a string of rooms in single file; in one instance the rooms extended around four sides of an open court, in the other in a straight line or bent into an L- or U-shape. Some houses at first may have had a simpler shape before being enlarged. This is true of Antonio Severino Martínez' house, which began as a dwelling of three rooms but was extended to thirteen after don Antonio acquired the property in 1824. On the other hand, numerous houses that today encompass only one or two sides of an open square may have once constituted a full hacienda.

Rooms built on a linear plan may or may not have intercommunicated. Each room had an outside door or window of some sort though only fairly important rooms had both since squared timber for woodwork was hard to come by. In all likelihood many openings between rooms were not closed with doors of wood but with hangings of fabric or hide (fig. 41).

One other arrangement of living spaces should be mentioned. A number of families occasionally banded together to create a "plaza," or fortified community. Each family built its string of rooms as described above, but placed them end to end. In this manner several houses could enclose a large central area of square or oblong shape. As in a hacienda, rooms opened toward the central area but the peripheral wall without openings created a defensible enceinte. Strong gates at one or more points barred entry to the plaza. Such defenses were absolutely essential for communities situated in the mountains (Las Trampas or Córdoba) or on the plains of the eastern frontier (Las Vegas, San Miguel). Even valley communities in the heart of Spanish territory sometimes banded together in this manner for mutual protection (Ranchos de Taos, Chimayó). Americans who visited the area described such arrangements as late as the 1850s. After American military posts brought Indian depredations under control the defenses were neglected and individual families began to disperse to more isolated locations adjacent to their fields. Today only one community—El Cerro de Chimayó, founded about 1730—retains its early closed form.

41 Simple houses probably had few interior doors and relied on cloth or hide hangings to close openings. The arches shown are not true arches, a feature practically unknown in colonial dwellings in New Mexico.

Rooms in Spanish buildings were of more or less uniform width (15 feet), although the length varied. With the possible exception of storage spaces, the largest, as well as the most elaborate, room of a dwelling was the *sala*, or parlor. Used for formal occasions, it contained more woodwork and a finished ceiling of *tablas* (short boards split from the sides of a log and placed so that the exposed surface was adzed and level), and because of its size, often two fireplaces. If the family owned such luxuries as mirrors or a bedstead, they probably were displayed here. Except for the *dispensa*, a storeroom guarded by a door with a stout lock and equipped with bins and chests containing wheat, meat, wine, and other provisions, there was little specialization of room use or design. The kitchen of big establishment, however, might have had an unusually large fireplace. If the owner of a house was engaged in trade with Chihuahua or the Midwest, he might use one or more rooms of his domicile for sales or storage. Basically each room was a rectangle equally inefficient for every purpose, and thus, it was not unusual for household activity to be shifted from room to room in search of a roof that leaked less than its neighbors. This changing use of rooms is well illustrated in the Palace of the Governors in Santa Fe, and it is one of the things that makes it very difficult to reconstruct the history of that building.

Ceilings were essentially alike, consisting of a primary system of logs spanning the room and supporting a secondary covering of smaller wooden members laid at right angles. If the sala was pretentious, the ceiling beams were adzed to a rectangular shape and supported on corbels, just as in some churches. The usual beam, however, was simply a log with the bark peeled off. The secondary covering in the sala might be made of tablas. Rooms of intermediate importance employed peeled aspen or cottonwood poles (*latias* or *savinos*) between the vigas. These poles were laid diagonally, or at right angles, to the vigas, and they might be split (in which case they were called *rajas*) or used in the round (figs. 42, 43, 44). It should also be noted that building terminology varies considerably from one section of the state to another. Construction materials employed for this layer of covering depended on what was available locally. Aspen poles were preferred because they were straight, fitted together closely, and were easily split. The difficulty of obtaining aspen, however, necessitated the use of cottonwood in the middle Rio Grande area and of willow in the south near Las Cruces. Ceilings of utilitarian rooms could be composed of split cedar, beautiful in appearance but inconvenient since wide cracks between the roughly fitted members allowed grains of dust from the earth covering to filter down when even slightly disturbed. In any case, a covering of brush or cedar bark was laid over secondary members before they were loaded with adobe to form the roof or the floor of the room above. Floors were earthen since boarding was extravagantly expensive. As late as 1848 no more than half a dozen structures in the whole territory had wood floors. Brick or tile were still not used for floors.

The fenestration of a colonial or Mexican house was totally unlike that of a

42 Ceiling of latias laid in a herring-bone pattern.

43 Ceiling of tablas, or short, adzed boards.

44 Ceiling of split cedar logs.

modern habitation—even if one attempts to imitate the earlier manner. Two factors explain this: the need for defense meant that window openings were quite small, and there was a total absence of window glass during the earlier periods. A very simple seventeenth- or eighteenth-century dwelling may have had no windows at all, depending entirely on a door for light and ventilation. When windows did exist they were customarily confined to one side of a room: in placita houses they faced the courtyard; in a linear house, the east or south elevation. Often the north wall was built against an embankment to give some degree of protection from winter storms. Windows on the end walls were always uncommon.

There were three types of fenestration: fixed sash, casement, or slabs of selenite built into the masonry. The simplest sash was a long, squat frame (approximately 8 x 15 inches) whose only filling was a series of stout wooden bars. Wood bars were used instead of iron because of the costliness of the latter; since nails were also expensive, the heavy frames were secured with mortise and tenon joints. Usually set high in the wall—often immediately under the roof supports—there was no way to close such openings except to stuff them with cloth or adobes. These windows were customarily used in barns and storerooms.

A cloth covering which transmitted little light but kept out the wind could be stretched over a frame to form another kind of fixed sash. As late as 1852 church accounts for Albuquerque, one of the major Spanish settlements in the Rio Abajo, refer to expenditures for lienzo, a kind of cotton cloth, to fill the sacristy windows. (Glass windows for this room were not added until 1869.) Selenite was also used in strips about 4 inches wide and as long as convenient. These were fitted into grooves cut in heavy wooden muntins of a fixed frame. Since it was not airtight, such a window was also provided with inside shutters to reduce drafts. One example still in place, though panes of glass have since been substituted for the original selenite, is found above the main entrance of the Santuario in Chimayó (fig. 45).

Early casement windows, which rotate on a vertical axis, could not have been very serviceable, particularly in winter when illumination was most needed, because they were constructed as a solid wooden shutter (fig. 46). The hinging action, obtained with pintles fitted into an independent frame, was similar to that of doors and will be explained later. Selenite panes set in muntins appear to have been too delicate for use in a hinged frame for no such casements survive.

Selenite, a crystallized gypsum that is translucent and abounds in the region, was mined in sheets up to 10 x 18 inches in size. Such sheets, like those in nineteenth-century houses at Zuñi, were "cemented" into the masonry with adobe plaster. It is ironic that the only extant examples of selenite windows, which were not used prior to Spanish occupation, are found in Indian edifices. While this material did not admit much light, it was more durable than cloth. Panels of selenite could be safely used in exterior walls inasmuch as Indian

45 Santuario at Chimayó, 1816. A fixed sash in which the narrow panes of selenite were fitted between the heavy vertical muntins; solid inside shutters also closed the opening.

46 Solid window with pintle hinges and mortice and tenon construction.

attacks consisted of short raids by mounted horsemen who did not venture too close to the building being attacked nor remain there long if they did approach it.

Examples of early fenestration are scarce. If a family was wealthy enough to maintain its home all these years, it could afford remodeling which included the addition of glass windows. But until the Americans began to import glass, that material remained virtually unknown in the region. One observant American soldier noted in 1846 that the only glass windows in the entire province were those in the Palace of the Governors in Santa Fe.

Doors, too, were not abundant. Because of the costliness of iron, which could only be secured from Mexico, latches, locks, and hinges were extremely rare. Lacking metal, local builders employed a pintle hinging device, one in which the ends of one vertical door stile, with the form of a round peg, were extended beyond the top and bottom rails. The pegs fitted into sockets sunk into the sill and the lintel supported the door and allowed it to rotate (fig. 47). Such a door must be installed when the lintel is put in place and cannot be removed without displacing the lintel. New Mexicans called such a door a *zambullo*, a type that can be traced back to early building practices in Mesopotamia and Egypt. In the absence of sawmills, lumber in the form of relatively thin boards was hard to obtain; it was easier to split and dress down a pine log in the form of a thick plank than a thin board. Customarily the stock out of which door rails and stiles were constructed was 2 to 2¾ inches thick. Panels might be as thin as 1¾ inches. Members were joined by means of mortises and tenons, but the fit was often crude. Very early examples seem to have consisted of a single vertical panel framed by four heavier members. Most common were those made with three rails and two panels. Some doors had a coarse molding cut into the framing with a plane, and panels were occasionally subdivided or in other instances enlivened with a crude raised design somewhat reminiscent of linenfold pattern. Another army officer, Lt. George Gibson, stationed in Santa Fe in 1846, observed doors in the Palace of the Governors covered with cow or buffalo hide, tanned, and painted to resemble wood.

A few doors of more elaborate design were made for churches or for important rooms in the homes of the rich. Composed of multiple panels put together to form a complex pattern, these doors recall seventeenth-century Baroque joinery in Spain, which had been inspired by Moorish work. The most famous example of this type of work is the pair of doors made in 1816 for the Santuario de Postrero in Chimayó (fig. 48). A variation of this design, in which some panels are replaced with turned spindles to provide for ventilation, was used for wall cupboards.

As observed earlier, Indians had adopted zambullo doors and windows in the course of the eighteenth and nineteenth centuries. Spanish doors generally were not as squat as Indian ones. They were, however, as low as five feet, and raised

47 Zambullo door, Penitente morada, Arroyo Hondo. The door is 4 feet, 11 inches high; the roughly hewn panels are 1.5 inches thick. Probably made as recently as 1852, but the technology employed here is characteristic of the colonial period.

48 Paneled door, Santuario at Chimayó, 1816. Representative of the most elaborate woodwork done in this area; an inscription in the upper panels dates this pair of doors 1816. Courtesy James M. Slack, HABS, Library of Congress.

sills were common. When such doors were installed in homes built in the 1920s, they often had to be lengthened to conform to modern ideas of comfort and safety. Before the advent of sawmills, doors of wood in ordinary New Mexican homes were undoubtedly rare, their place being taken by skin or textile coverings.

One other type of door must be mentioned. That is the *portón*, the heavy gate of two leaves that closed the zaguán or the plaza and was stout enough to withstand an armed attack. Each leaf was between 3½ feet and 4 feet wide and about 8 feet high. Unfortunately no eighteenth-century examples appear to have survived. It is likely that they turned on pintles as do surviving church doors with about the same dimensions, but whether they had a paneled construction or were built up of two layers of wood, as were gates of later date, is not known.

The best surviving portón comes from a house near Ranchos de Taos that belonged to an American named Horace Long (fig. 49). Although Long did not come to the area until 1839, the house and its gate could have been built earlier. (Records of real estate transactions for that period have been lost or were not kept.) At any rate, this gate is constructed of two layers of boards, each 1 5/16 inches thick, and held together by hundreds of spikes whose points were flattened against the inner surface. Instead of pintles, each leaf turns on iron truncheons supported by hinges forged in the shape of half circles. Whether these hinges were made in Mexico, or in New Mexico from imported iron, is a matter of conjecture. One leaf contains a wicket, common in Mexico and Spain, to be used by pedestrians when the heavy portal is closed. Because of their weight, such gates were hard to keep in repair, and when the Indian menace diminished most were allowed to deteriorate.

Although no type of carved stone or stucco ornamentation was known in the province, a New Mexico exterior sometimes had one point of embellishment, the

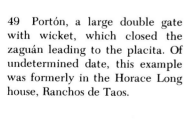

49 Portón, a large double gate with wicket, which closed the zaguán leading to the placita. Of undetermined date, this example was formerly in the Horace Long house, Ranchos de Taos.

portal, or covered porch. Normally this feature was located on the south or east side of a simple building, at the intersection of the arms of an L- or U-shaped one, or within the placita of a hacienda. The portal consisted of a long beam run parallel to the façade and, depending on its length, supported by two or more posts. If the beam was anchored in a wall, a post at that point might be omitted. The beam, generally trimmed to a rectangular shape, supported a system of vigas of rounded shapes and smaller size. The latter were often 15 feet in length, the customary width of a room. Between the principal beam and vertical posts supporting it were usually interposed horizontal corbel brackets or *zapatas,* as they are called in Mexico (fig. 50). Structurally these members can be explained as a transitional device for increasing the bearing area of the post, but sometimes in New Mexico the main beam and zapatas were a single piece, from the same log. This demonstrates both the abundance of large timbers in northern New Mexico and the curious lack of engineering understanding of the builders. In some cases the front surface of the zapata was ornamented with simple chiseled geometric designs on the flat surface, but there was never anything in the way of modeling or carved relief. In a more elaborately carved form, the zapata is a familiar element in Mexican as well as in Spanish building of the Renaissance and Middle Ages, and its origins can be traced back at least as far as the Islamic period.

The interior of a colonial house was as simple as its exterior. Walls were surfaced with the same type of mud plaster whose color depended on what clay was available locally, though a lighter appearance could be obtained by using a finish coat of whitish clay. To obtain this material, home decorators would sometimes travel many miles. When this was impractical, a homemade calcimine called *jaspe* was frequently employed. Since jaspe brushed off easily, a protecting dado of calico was often hung along the lower part of the wall, a practice which became prevalent after the opening of the Santa Fe Trail. In other Spanish interiors a dado of dark-colored mud plaster, similar to that used earlier by the Indians, was employed.

Floors were earthen, in some instances sealed with a thin coating composed of clay and animal blood. These simple interior surfaces made the inside clean-cut and clearly defined. Still, irregularities in the wall surfaces and of the undulating corners formed by deeply recessed windows and doors gave these interiors an effective sculptural quality.

The single point of architectural interest in a room, aside from this lively sense of geometry, was the *fogón* or fireplace. Most often it was in a corner and had a low—6 to 8 inches—hearth. Usually it was roughly quarter round in plan, had a narrow (approximately 20 inches) parabola-shaped opening, a shallow firebox, a pronounced mantel, and a square projecting flue set into the corner (fig. 51). The firebox was so small that logs had to be placed in an upright position, but the thermal efficiency was surprisingly good. If one fogón was deemed

50 A portal like this from Las Córdobas could have been made any time between 1700 and 1860. This beam and zapatas are cut from a single log (U.S. Soil Conservation Service, No. 114–G–NM–10,803 in the National Archives, Washington, D.C.).

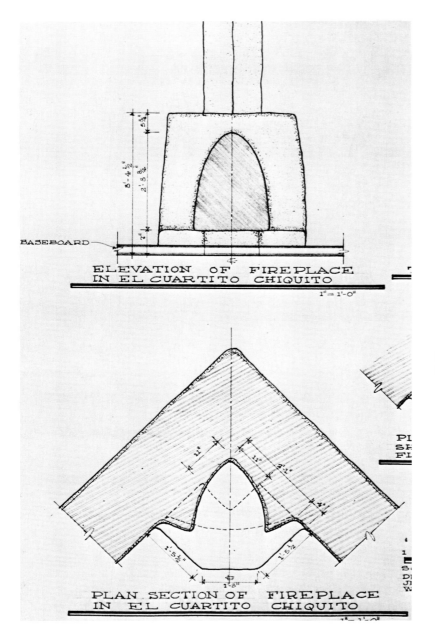

ELEVATION OF FIREPLACE
IN EL CUARTITO CHIQUITO

1" = 1'-0"

BASEBOARD

PLAN SECTION OF FIREPLACE
IN EL CUARTITO CHIQUITO

51 Measured drawing of a typical fireplace from a house dated about 1870, in Peñasco.

insufficient for a room of large dimensions, a second was added in the opposite corner. The arch of the opening was formed by using two large adobe bricks of half-parabola shape which had been especially cast and dried before being set in place. The chimney was small, about 10 x 10 inches, had no damper, and its walls were constructed of unusually thin (2 to 2½ inches) adobe bricks set on edge with ends fitted into vertical channels cut in the walls of the room. Burned brick, it will be remembered, was not then available for lining the firebox or flue, but fortunately, there was little danger from fire in an edifice where walls, roofs, and floors were constructed of clay. An even simpler (and perhaps earlier) form of corner fireplace was formed by constructing a light hood over the hearth. No good Spanish examples survive, perhaps because of the flimsy construction, but fogónes of this type were still in use at Zuñi in 1880. (See figs. 52–56.)

Evidence of corner fireplaces dating from the seventeenth century, however, has been found. Gran Quivira, the Franciscan convent, begun in 1659 and constructed of ledge stone rather than adobe, is well preserved even though it was abandoned in the 1670s because of the raids by Plains Indians. One room in the convent contains the remains of a corner fireplace in which the ends of a curved log are still fitted into the stone masonry. As in a fireplace recorded by Mindeleff at Zuñi, this log would have supported a light plastered hood. A second fireplace exists in the neighboring mission station, comparable in date and also abandoned, of Quarai. Built entirely of stone and situated in a corner, its small opening is spanned by a triangular "arch" made of two stones set at an angle.

Where a more ample hearth was required, as in the kitchen of a large household, the opening was made larger (up to 4 feet, 4 inches) and the firebox was covered with a bell-shaped hood; hence the term *fogón de campana*. An unusual fireplace still survives in the José Gregorio Valdez house in Taos. It has two openings set at right angles to each other, with the spanning arches supported on a cylindrical pier, and the whole covered by the usual bell-shaped hood.

If a builder wished to locate a hearth against the middle of a wall rather than in a corner, he constructed a low spur parapet, a *paredcito*, at right angles to the wall and then constructed the usual kind of fireplace in the resulting corner.

One other type of fireplace did exist. It was constructed with a beam run parallel to the rear wall of the room and supported by the side walls. The space between the beam and the wall was covered with a series of contiguous poles, *latias*, similar in appearance and function to ceiling construction. The poles were plastered over with mud to form a storage shelf which might sometimes have been used also as a bed—hence the popular name, "shepherd's bed" fireplace. Above the shelf, in one corner, a smoke hood was built of poles or thin adobes set vertically as described above. The fire was kindled in the corner on the low hearth, but there was no firebox to contain it. Only two examples of this arrangement have survived.

All these hearths were low (6 to 8 inches), and we lack any evidence that New Mexico builders ever employed counter-high hearths for kitchens, despite the popularity of this form in Mexico and Spain. Fray Francisco Atanasio Domínguez, whom we know to be an accurate reporter, does, however, make it clear that charcoal burners were employed in the kitchens of some New Mexico convents during the late eighteenth century. As none have survived, or been identified in excavations, we do not know their exact form, but they may have had the familiar stove-like shape of small burners set into a masonry bench or table at waist height. Like its prototype in Spain and Mexico, the burner was

52 A corner fireplace under construction in an unknown location. Notice that the adobe brick in the chimney has been laid vertically (U.S. Soil Conservation Service, No. 114–G−NM−7,138 in the National Archives, Washington, D.C.).

53   Corner fireplace lintel, Humanas mission, 1659. The curved lintel embedded in both walls supported a light hood of sticks or corn stalks plastered on both sides.

54 Bell-shaped fireplace used in large kitchens. This is from a Penitente morada, Arroyo Hondo, and is dated between 1852 and 1856.

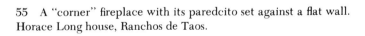

55 A "corner" fireplace with its paredcito set against a flat wall. Horace Long house, Ranchos de Taos.

56 Unusually large corner fireplace, or fogón de campana, in the José Gregorio Valdez house, Taos, 1834.

probably placed under a plastered smoke hood of light construction, which it probably shared with the regular fireplace. Thus the cook might prepare food on open fires during the winter when extra heat was needed, and on charcoal at other times. When iron cook stoves were brought in from the United States, they replaced the earlier, less convenient cooking arrangements. Such fireplaces as do remain, therefore, were probably not located in rooms generally used as kitchens.

Other than doors, windows, ceilings, and fireplaces, the only other interior feature of note was the recessed wall cupboard. When the cupboard had doors they probably contained some turned spindles. A simpler arrangement for storage consisted of a heavy plank set high against a wall and extending the full width of the room. In a sense, this was the counterpart of the hanging pole found in Zuñi interiors already discussed.

The preceding paragraphs dealing with domestic buildings of the Spanish and Mexican periods have been general in nature, based largely on scraps of information pieced together or from literary references. The reason for this is that no old unremodeled houses survive. The nearest thing to a colonial domicile is the Antonio Severino Martínez house, built largely between 1824 and 1827, on the Taos River some four miles below Taos Pueblo. Although features from this edifice have been cited frequently in the preceding paragraphs as illustrations of colonial building practices, this structure has been repeatedly modified, most recently in 1975–76. One other secular structure which has enjoyed almost continuous occupancy since it was begun in 1610, is the Palace of the Governors in Santa Fe (fig. 57). It has, however, been so often and so heavily remodeled that it is difficult to visualize its original appearance. Excavations on the palace carried out in 1973–75 by the staff of the Museum of New Mexico, have provided more questions than answers. In the seventeenth century the palace housed the governor and his household, the provincial administrative offices, the jail, and the military garrison. It was an enormous building, much longer than the present palace, which still occupies the entire north side of the plaza. Consisting of extensive storerooms, corrals, and walled gardens, it occupied the whole area between the present plaza and the Federal Building two blocks to the north. Sturdy defense towers stood at each end of the main façade, the one at the east end fitted out on the interior as a chapel. Adjacent to it was a gateway that pierced the town walls on the east. Sometime before 1837 the eastern tower was demolished and a wooden portal added; the western tower, which contained the prison, was taken down in 1866 when Lincoln Avenue was laid out. Since American occupation the façade has three times been drastically modified and in 1976 is being restored. Considering that the projecting towers at each end of the façade were erected to protect the face of the building from assault, it is unlikely that originally there was a portal which might have furnished assailants with shelter.

Today only that portion of the building fronting the plaza is old, those to the rear and sides having been largely rebuilt in the early part of this century. This old section is two rooms deep, though a few rooms or halls carry across the building. The double-file plan contrasts with the single-file standard for private dwellings in colonial New Mexico although a double plan is found in the Governor's Palace built in 1749, at San Antonio, Texas. This latter building has also been much restored. The double-file plan, of course, allows for somewhat more privacy and flexibility of use, but to what extent this arrangement is original in Santa Fe is a question that cannot yet be answered. Recent excavations have revealed the presence of wall foundations running parallel to the façade about 15 feet inside (south of) the rear wall of the building. Though excavations have only been carried out in three rooms, they suggest that the present room arrangement may not be original.

57 Portal of the Palace of the Governors, Santa Fe, after the 1867–68 remodeling. Photograph ca. 1890, by Ben Wittick.

The palace has had a lively history. At the time of the 1680 Revolt all Spaniards who were able made their way to the palace and there defended themselves against the Indian attacks until the latter diverted the ditch that supplied water. At that point the embattled Spaniards fought their way out of the palace and made their way to El Paso. Upon reconquest in 1693, they found Indians living in parts of the palace. Recent excavations have revealed the presence of storage cists and fire pits which may date from that occupancy. Ironically, the Spanish expelled the Indian inhabitants, using the same means by which they had been ousted—cutting off the water supply. The chapel in the east tower had been profaned and was not reconsecrated. Instead a separate church for the military was erected on the opposite (south) side of the plaza. Within the palace many roofs had to be replaced and much damage repaired. But as late as 1846, when the Americans arrived, there was not a wooden floor in the building and roofs, even those covering rooms in which state archives were stored, were in wretched repair. However, glass windows had already replaced colonial fenestration in a few rooms.

As stated, no specialized civil or commercial architecture existed in New Mexico, since all types of activity were carried on with about equal inconvenience in a standard dwelling. With one exception, there was no specialized military architecture beyond the fortified "plazas." That exception is the *torreón*, a fortified tower, generally two stories high. After the Reconquest, the Spanish erected a number of these towers, generally in the vicinity of a cluster of small ranches. The crown proposed a string of such towers, separated by distances of one day's travel, along the trail leading to El Paso. It was thought that these could be used by travelers or by refugees in case of another revolt. Today only one torreón remains, that belonging to the Antonio José Vigil family in Talpa near Ranchos de Taos (fig. 58). The remains of two more stand in Dixon (formerly called Embudo), and fine examples are known to have existed in Manzano and Los Córdobas as recently as the 1930s. The torreón was round and had an interior diameter of about 15 feet, the usual span of a room. Its adobe or stone walls were 2 to 3 feet thick. There was one stout door, and one or more small windows placed high and barred with a wooden grill. A fireplace is hollowed out of the wall in one Embudo example. Here women and children sought safety in case of emergency. The ceiling was covered in the regular manner but there was a trapdoor giving access to the upper level, from which male defenders might fight off attackers. Torreones have been reconstructed in Lincoln and at Las Golondrinas Ranch near La Ciénega with second-story walls of adobe. One señor Vigil, owner of the sole surviving torreón maintains, however, that he remembers log construction on the upper level of his torreón. This would make sense, as the overhanging corners of the polygonal log superstructure would provide space for loopholes for firing down vertically upon attackers who had moved in against the walls. (Domínguez comments on the perils of being trapped inside a torreón by attacking Indians.) The splendid torreón at Manzano, demolished in 1939 by the State Highway Department, communicated by door with a contiguous room; the same may have been true of one torreón at Dixon, as well as of the early towers on the Palace of the Governors.

One other building type requires some discussion: structures constructed of log. Buildings of this genre are confined to communities in the mountains since in New Mexico trees large enough for building purposes do not thrive below elevations of about 7500 feet. It should be noted that in communities like Las Trampas or Truchas, although timber was abundant, adobe was preferred for dwellings and timber was utilized only for service structures—barns, shelters, corrals, storage sheds, and grist mills. Depending on the weather-tightness required, the logs were trimmed and the joints chinked. Where a tight interior was needed, the logs would also be plastered with mud on exterior as well as interior surfaces, and in some instances it is therefore difficult to distinguish the appearance of a log from an adobe edifice. The attached storage shed of a house in Las Trampas is constructed of log, the house of adobe (fig. 59). Grist mills form an important class of log construction (fig. 60). Here walls and substructure were of timber because the location adjacent to a mill race was a poor place for adobe. Moisture splashed from the mill wheel, or seepage from the ditch embankment, would soon have caused disintegration. Since, however, it was necessary that the

58 Torreón of the Antonio José Vigil family, Talpa, New Mexico.

59 Adobe house with attached storeroom (foreground) built of logs but plastered to conform to the rest of the house. Typical log barns and storage sheds in rear with board-on-board roofs.

60 Grist mill on Taos River mentioned in the 1827 will of Antonio Severino Martínez. The holes in the ends of the roughly squared logs were cut to facilitate dragging them down from the forest. Photographed in 1901, the building is no longer standing.

grinding area be tightly sealed, the logs were squared and fitted with particular care and the interior wall surfaces as well as the floor were mud plastered.

It has long been taken for granted that log construction spread to New Mexico from the English and French colonies on the east coast. Recent investigation by Professor Charles Gritzner of the methods used for notching the logs, as well as the fact that the horizontal water wheel rotated counterclockwise as was the custom in Latin countries, indicate that this technology was undoubtedly brought from Mexico by early colonists. The customary ridge or shed roofs constructed of boards, however, would appear to be a post-Hispanic addition since the latter were not much used before the introduction of sawmills.

In addition to structures in which the logs were laid horizontally, there was some use of jacal construction which placed members vertically. The latter was used for corral construction where the posts were embedded to a substantial depth in the ground. A lighter construction using vertical poles set in the earth, spaced several inches apart, bound together with rawhide and possibly interlaced with reeds or brush, was used to make chicken pens and the like. Interesting evidence of such construction has been uncovered in the recent (1975, 1976) excavations at Carnué, a farming outpost located just east of Albuquerque which flourished briefly in the 1760s. It is also likely that the Spanish employed non-bearing walls of wattle and daub for temporary shelters or for partitions in rooms, though none have survived. Such usage would not have differed greatly from the light wattle-and-daub construction used in early Indian times; it is, however, substantially different from a sturdier jacal which will be discussed in the next section.

4

ARCHITECTURE
OF THE EARLY AMERICAN PERIOD

Revolutionary changes in the culture of New Mexico, caused by the influx of American settlers and ideas during the nineteenth century, are recorded by the region's architecture. American influence was slight when the Santa Fe Trail opened in 1821, increased after annexation in 1848, and became major after the arrival of the railroad in 1880. The changes were of many kinds. The technology of the area was drastically altered by the introduction of new tools and methods brought from the States. The Roman Catholic Church, under the leadership of Bishop Jean Baptiste Lamy, was subjected to important reforms. There was a marked improvement in the region's economy, especially after the extension of the railroad to the Rio Grande Valley. And nomadic Indians, who had long harassed the Pueblo and Spanish occupants of the area, were permanently brought under control. Indeed, the sixty-four years between 1848 and 1912, the date New Mexico became a state, witnessed much more change than had the previous two and a half centuries.

Trade with the States began with the opening of the Santa Fe Trail in 1821 and grew steadily in importance. In 1825, 34 wagons reached New Mexico; by 1843, the number was 175. After the Civil War, of course, the length of the journey made by wagon (800 miles) was gradually reduced as the railhead of the Atchison Topeka and Santa Fe Railroad was pushed steadily westward. Under Spanish rule New Mexico had been starved for consumer goods since the price of even the simplest article obtained through Mexico City and Chihuahua was far beyond the means of an average person. Following Mexican independence when American traders ventured into the Southwest, they were well rewarded financially. The first cargoes contained small, practical items: needles and thread, bolts of cloth, axes, guns, and staples such as coffee and spirits. After annexation, inventories became more varied and included hand tools, iron plows, machinery for simple manufacturing purposes, and nursery products. In this way, New Mexico slowly became more productive and self-sustaining. The army, for example, set up a sawmill in Santa Fe in 1848 and soon portable steam-powered mills were active in various parts of the region. Midwestern nurserymen traveled to the area selling plants and fruit trees and taking orders for delivery the following year. After the completion of the railroad, however, the region was flooded with American goods of all varieties which soon overwhelmed native crafts produced in all but the most remote portions of the territory. Of particular interest is how thoroughly this flood of goods revolutionized the technology of the region and in turn radically affected the architecture.

Change of quite a different order occurred in the organization and administration of the Catholic Church, heretofore the most stable institution in the region. On the initiative of U.S. Roman Catholic leaders, New Mexico was separated in 1851 from the Mexican Diocese of Durango and placed under the authority of a French priest, Jean Baptiste Lamy. Lamy was soon made bishop of the new diocese. Following the Mexican War of Independence, the church in New Mexico had been neglected by the Mexican government; friars of Spanish birth had been expelled and many missions and parishes left empty. Whereas as many as sixty-six priests had served the province in the eighteenth century, in 1850, when Lamy arrived, only fourteen priests were left in New Mexico. Within a few years he had filled the vacancies with priests brought from the Midwest, and together they embarked on a vigorous campaign of ecclesiastical reform as well as repair of neglected church edifices.

An important new element in New Mexican life was added by the large numbers of American settlers who moved here following annexation, especially after the Civil War. Whereas an estimated 36,000 Americans lived in New Mexico in 1850, there were perhaps as many as 51,000 in 1880. (United States census figures for that period do not differentiate between language groups, only between the literate and illiterate.) The Americans' understanding and appreciation of the culture and customs they encountered were not noteworthy. By and large they regarded the native population as unprogressive, and their only goal was to transplant the American Midwest to the Rio Grande as completely and as rapidly as possible. The prompt appearance of the Territorial style of architecture illustrates in visual terms to what degree they succeeded. It is important to point out that this symbol of "progress" was readily accepted also by the Spanish population of the area.

Economic progress under American domination is striking and it contrasts with the stagnation of the previous centuries. Basically, it was due to two things: improved and less expensive transportation which permitted New Mexican products in quantity for the first time to move to eastern markets, and the ultimate subjugation of the nomadic Indians. The latter permitted the expansion of agriculture, cattle raising, and mining into vast areas not previously exploited.

The architectural counterpart of these changes was a striking departure from the conservative Spanish-Pueblo tradition so long unchallenged in the region. The new type of architecture, the Territorial style, can be divided into three phases: the first extended from 1848 to 1865, the second from that date to sometime after 1880, and the third between 1880 and 1912. Although it developed a unique form in New Mexico, the Territorial style should be identified as a belated extension of the Greek Revival manner which had flourished on the eastern seaboard between about 1820 and 1850. The parent style had moved westward through the South and Midwest until it reached New Mexico. That it did not come to New Mexico from Mexico is certain since no structures with comparable motifs exist in northern or central Mexico. The full force of Neo-Classic architecture never extended into Mexico because the War of Independence discouraged building.

EARLY TERRITORIAL, 1848–1865

No unmodified architectural examples from this phase of the movement are extant so that information about it must be pieced together from surviving fragments and early photographs. The most important buildings of this period were situated in the centers of Santa Fe and Las Vegas. In the villages along the Santa Fe Trail, which must also have had some good examples, buildings have all but disappeared for the same reasons that colonial buildings did so. Furthermore, exact information as to dates of construction in this period is lacking. It is probable, however, that the first signs of Territorial work appeared in the mid–1850s since the most important ingredients for the style—sawn lumber and window glass—were by then available. One important exception is the Clawson house in San Miguel del Vado, the town at which the Santa Fe Trail crossed the Pecos River. Although no record survives of the early owner of this large dwelling, tree-ring analysis marks its construction date as 1855.

A characteristic trademark of the Territorial style is the pedimented lintel used over doors and windows. The earliest form of this feature may have been fairly simple, lacking moldings. One early example is seen in some of the windows and door frames of the Clawson house (fig. 61), as well as in those of the Palace of the Governors in Santa Fe. Later window trim becomes more complex with members built up of several sections of molding added to the facia, as in the old schoolhouse in Albuquerque (fig. 62). It should be noted, however, that plain facing boards to frame openings are common in modest structures during the entire Territorial era and do not in themselves signify an early date. Another characteristic of early Territorial millwork is the use of fairly heavy (6 x 6 inches)

61   Early Territorial trim was simple, as on the Clawson house, San Miguel del Vado, 1855.

62   Later Territorial trim was more elaborate, built up of several pieces of molding, as demonstrated by that on the old Court House, Old Town, Albuquerque, 1878. Here the cement plaster was scored to simulate ashlar masonry.

portal posts with chamfered corners. When lumber had to be transported some distance, 4 x 4 posts were used. Timbers destined for use as ceiling beams were sawn into rectangular sections enlivened with corner bead moldings. Photographs of Santa Fe Plaza in the early days indicate that the wood trim of structures was painted white in the manner of the Greek Revival elsewhere. The early Territorial movement introduced no important construction changes; walls continued to be made of adobe brick and roofs remained flat and earth-packed.

The first Territorial features probably appeared when an earlier building was remodeled—a new window with glass was inserted or an old zambullo door replaced by one that fitted better and turned on metal hinges. When a space larger than that provided by the usual 15-foot wide colonial room was needed (as, for example, in a store) longer mill-sawn joists could be obtained.

MIDDLE TERRITORIAL, 1865–1880

The most characteristic Territorial architecture belongs to the years 1865–80, and it is work from this period that one generally visualizes when thinking of the style. The full force of the movement developed when commerce with the States revived after the Civil War: a pervading optimism encouraged secular building on an unprecedented scale, and construction also received impetus from new building at numerous military forts. The first forts, established in the 1850s to contain the nomadic Indians, had been crude, temporary affairs made of logs; but most of their replacements in the late 1860s were built of adobe and had glass windows and rather elaborate wooden trim (fig. 63). Comfortable officers' quarters undoubtedly inspired neighboring ranchers and townspeople to seek for themselves more up-to-date, American-style homes. The same can be said of the effect of the sutters' stores or headquarters buildings on territorial merchants.

Compared to the colonial era, this period had a greater variety of building types, even if not of construction methods. Housebuilding continued to dominate construction activity. In addition to remodeling, which continued to be important, new homes were built in increasing numbers, and generally they followed a new plan. This plan was symmetrical based on a center hall or room, and it was two or more rooms deep, in contrast to the old single-file plan of colonial times (fig. 64). Buildings opened outward, especially to the front where a porch was often located—a change made practical after the Indian threat had been eliminated. Correlative to this was elimination of the placita. Residences of two stories—especially on large ranches—became more common. Indeed, the New Mexican idea of a mansion in the decades following the Civil War appears to have consisted of a two-story dwelling with a verandah, also of two levels. The finest examples (like Los Luceros) had verandahs on all four sides (fig. 65).

63 Quartermasters Depot, Fort Union, illustrates characteristic Greek Revival–Territorial design of post–Civil War military installations in New Mexico. Photograph, probably 1868 (U.S. Signal Corps, No. 111–SC–88,008 in the National Archives, Washington, D.C.).

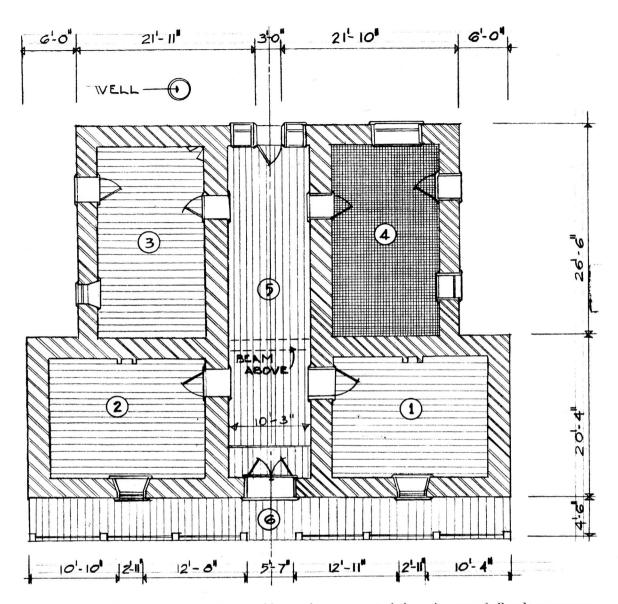

64 Characteristic Territorial house plan, symmetrical about the center hall and two or more rooms deep. Leandro Martínez house, Taos, 1862.

The symmetrical organization of rooms was reflected in the fenestration. Although casements were sometimes used, double-hung sashes were more common. Each unit was divided into six or nine panes. (Panes increased in size as freighting across the plains became more routine.) Window casings were elaborate, both inside and out, with facings customarily enlivened by applied moldings of some kind. Interior jambs, often splayed, were paneled, and sometimes windows were equipped with interior shutters. Exterior blinds were also frequently used.

The entrance was the building's most elaborate feature. Side lights flanking the door, and often an overlight as well, were common (fig. 66). In many

65   Los Luceros, a characteristic Territorial hacienda with a double portal surrounding the building.

66   The unusually "pure" (for New Mexico) Greek Revival woodwork of Phoenix Ranch headquarters building was probably done by carpenters from nearby Fort Union.

instances the entrances are so well done, by Greek Revival standards, that they could be midwestern. The square (usually 4 x 4 inches) posts that supported the entrance porch had corner bead moldings and were generally accented by heavier horizontal moldings with mitred corners applied to each face at top and bottom in an effort to recall Classical capitals and bases. These moldings were cut by hand.

Not infrequently walls were capped with three to six courses of kiln-baked brick. These were laid so that some headers projected alternately or were set at a forty-five-degree angle to recall dentils; other courses projected uniformly to imitate the crown of a cornice. Burned brick, which at first had to be hauled from Fort Leavenworth, Kansas, served the useful function of preventing erosion along the top of the adobe wall. The manufacture of brick in New Mexico did not begin until the 1880s. Bricks were also employed to construct chimney flues, fireboxes, and hearths. In some pretentious buildings in Las Vegas and Santa Fe, the adobe walls were covered with cement plaster, scored with a rectangular pattern to recall stone masonry. Such efforts were undoubtedly considered very "progressive" and "American."

Interior fittings were more elaborate. Wood floors became commonplace, and since they were pine, some rooms were even carpeted. Inasmuch as milled lumber was available, the ceilings were frequently framed with rectangular beams cut with crisp bead moldings. Boarding of random lengths covered the roof joists, in contrast to the colonial latias or hand-adzed tablas which only spanned a single bay, but like their predecessors, they were covered over with earth to provide insulation and keep out moisture. To keep dirt from filtering down from the roof, *manta*, a heavy cotton cloth, was often tacked to the underside of the ceiling beams. When painted with a mixture of flour and water, this material shrank and somewhat resembled a plaster ceiling. Doors between rooms were usual, and they rotated on metal hinges rather than wooden pintles. Fine homes might even boast double doors to connect parlors. Fireplaces in important rooms were cased with wooden chimney breasts and, though the hearth retained the traditional elliptical opening and plan, it was more frequently placed flat against the wall rather than in a corner (fig. 67). Wall cupboards, trimmed with wood and often provided with paneled doors, were not uncommon.

A new type of structure that developed along with trade on the Santa Fe Trail was the retail store. These were larger and better lighted than colonial sales rooms which were usually nothing more than a room in the merchant's dwelling. The new stores were frequently provided with ample double entrance doors and furnished with counters and shelves. Rooms usually exceeded the standard colonial 15-foot width and show windows composed of numerous panes were common. Often store buildings were two stories, with the upper level used for offices, a hotel, or the residence of the owner. Although at a later date, space for

67   The traditional corner fireplace provided with Territorial wood trim and mantel shelf.

the stairs to the second floor was reserved on the façade, the earliest staircases appear to have been located on the rear or flank of the building. The roof of the customary portal covering the sidewalk in front of the store served as a terrace for second-floor rooms. Sometimes the terrace also was covered with a roof supported by posts, thereby creating a portal of two levels resembling those found on the more ambitious haciendas. In an interesting variation (still preserved in several stores in Las Vegas and Santa Fe and in one in Socorro) the second-floor porch took the form of a balcony cantilevered from the building or supported on wooden brackets. Roofing depended on the placement of the building on its lot: if contiguous with other structures, the low pitch drained to the rear; if freestanding, it was generally capped by a hip roof. False fronts, so characteristic of the West, do not seem to have been employed in Territorial designs of this period. They did make an appearance later—in imitation of the masonry façades with fancy pressed metal cornices that came in the wake of the railroad.

The years 1865–85 saw the remodeling and building of many new churches. Protestant congregations began to grow and by the early 1870s some were able to build permanent quarters. The most elaborate of these was that erected by the

Presbyterians in Old Las Vegas in 1871. Undoubtedly the pride of the congregation, and of most progress-minded settlers, was the portico of this church (fig. 68). Employing columns two stories tall, and capped by a gable treated as a pediment, this was the only attempt in the territory at a Classical temple front. Instead of being round, the columns were square, made by four boards nailed together. The door and window trim executed by David Powell is also elaborate. (From the sparse references available it appears that the more expert carpenters usually were American, or perhaps it was they who had the better tools.) Characteristic of Territorial entrance compositions, the fairly elaborate door of the church was achieved by simple means: plain boards and a dentil course, made from sections of a cyma reversa molding, were tacked to the frame. They recall an architrave capped by a cornice and have a scale that is heavy enough to dominate the composition (fig. 69). A second dentil course of slightly smaller scale enlivens the lintel that separates the door from the overlight. The vertical boards that case the door were converted into pilasters by the addition of nicely mitred moldings which suggest capitals. The jambs and soffit of the doorframe set into the two-foot thick adobe wall were paneled, and for one of the few times in this whole chapter of frontier building, some correspondence was maintained between paneling in the frame and the doors. The church interior consisted of an entrance vestibule, a large (55 x 26 feet) auditorium, and a Sunday school room, all combined within a rectangular outline. A house for the minister was built next door.

Architectural undertakings by Catholics were more numerous and of greater variety. Although work on churches themselves usually followed a Folk Gothic form, that for associated buildings could be of Territorial style. Good examples of these were the Territorial rectory, convent, and school erected in Albuquerque adjacent to the eighteenth-century church, which, during exactly the same years (1870–80), was remodeled in a provincial Gothic fashion. The school in particular is important and contains one of the handsomest Territorial doors in the state. The dentil course is carved from a single board, not tacked on, while the volutes and acanthus leaves of the capitals were carved separately out of three-quarter-inch boards and ingeniously fitted together in rough approximation of the Corinthian order (fig. 70). Unfortunately, building accounts for the school are not preserved, but an oral tradition still current in the 1930s said that this doorframe was made by an Italian carpenter who had settled in Albuquerque.

The construction of several military forts in the late 1860s and early 1870s represented a major architectural undertaking for the territory. Unfortunately almost nothing remains of this type of building since the forts were deactivated by the 1890s after the power of the Apache and Navajo tribes had been broken. The abandoned buildings were ransacked by neighboring ranchers for structural timbers or firewood. The adobe walls were left to deteriorate so that for the most part only ruins survive. Fort Marcy in Santa Fe, the oldest and probably the most

68 Presbyterian church and manse, West Las Vegas, 1871. This represents the only attempt at a classical temple front during the Territorial period. The bell tower, which is out of scale and character, is contemporary with the building.

69 Entrance, Presbyterian church, West Las Vegas, 1871. The wood-work for this building was done by David H. Powell.

elaborate of the group, has been overrun by the city. Fortunately, the U.S. Army Signal Corps photographed the forts while they were still in use. Pleasant, straightforward, and vernacular, this Greek Revival work was certainly old-fashioned by eastern standards at the time of construction. Some roofs were flat, but others such as the officers' houses and base hospital in Santa Fe were pitched and sheathed with terneplate or shingles.

A nice aspect of all this construction was the large windows, both casement and double hung. As observed earlier, the officers' quarters at these forts probably did much to influence the domestic architecture of New Mexico in the years following the Civil War. As might be expected, the barracks, shops, storehouses, and corrals were simpler in design, but all had ample fenestration. While the glass, wooden moldings, and fired brick were freighted in from the Midwest, lumber for finished work as well as framing was obtained in New Mexico as one can see from advertisements in the regional newspapers.

Worth mentioning is the fact that these stations were fortified only to the extent that some corrals and supply yards were enclosed by buildings as a deterrent to theft. In only two instances were earthen defense works constructed, at Fort Marcy and at Fort Union, both of which were erected in anticipation of an attack by Confederate troops. At Fort Union, when the larger, permanent, third fort was constructed in the late 1860s on a new site, most buildings were

70 Palace of the Governors, Santa Fe. The chronology of the nineteenth-century remodelings and photographs have not yet been worked out. This portal was probably erected between 1855 and 1860 (U.S. Signal Corps, No. 111–SC–87,933 in the National Archives, Washington, D.C.).

spaced around a large parade ground. The reason for this lack of defensive precautions was that the large installations were never subject to Indian assault. Most military engagements were fought in Indian territory.

In addition to forts, churches, stores, and houses, a fair number of civic buildings were erected or remodeled during the Territorial period. The most notable is the Palace of the Governors in Santa Fe. In wretched condition in 1846, it has been subjected to an almost continuous process of remodeling ever since. Setting aside internal changes, which would constitute another study, the exterior of the palace underwent two major modifications in territorial times. The first, executed most likely in the mid-1850s, added a rather plain portal of heavy posts with a minimum of applied molding; a second in 1868–78 fancied up the first endeavor with a new balustrade and more trim. The window and doorframes on the exterior are of two designs and possibly date from different building campaigns. Most of the inside trim, both simple and with quite elaborate paneling, was unfortunately defaced and plastered over when the palace was "colonialized" between 1909 and 1914. In 1976 some of it is being restored.

A new stone structure to house federal offices was projected in 1853, but work was suspended because of the Civil War. When construction resumed in 1882, the design was updated by Victorian standards. Had it been completed according to the original scheme sent out from Washington, it would have been the one legitimate Greek Revival structure in the territory.

Before moving on to the railroad era, mention should be made of certain sectional differences discernible in the architecture dating from the last third of the century. Most of these distinctions were caused by the availability of materials locally. In mountain villages, for example, where rainfall is plentiful and good stands of timber handy, ridge and hip roofs appear to have been in common and early use, perhaps before the Civil War. These roofs were covered with shingles, lapped boards, or board over board. Despite their somewhat light construction, they were sufficiently steep (about 7 in 10) to shed rainfall, but an old-fashioned flat roof of earth always lay below the pitched one to provide insulation. In later years when corrugated iron became available, it replaced the exposed boarding. In the area from Santa Fe south where some structural timber had to be hauled in, roofs remained flat as in colonial times. Here the adobe parapets were capped with several courses of fired brick as described earlier. Though a good stand of timber grew in the mountains immediately north of Santa Fe, the supply was apparently not sufficient for roofing as well as for more fundamental structural purposes so that flat roofs continued to be used there.

In southern New Mexico, around Old Mesilla and Doña Ana, which are long distances from pine forests, large straight logs were so scarce that it was not uncommon to find a zaguán entry spanned by an arch of adobe rather than by a lintel. Although small arches had been employed in the early eighteenth-century church at Pecos Pueblo, they appear not to have been used again until late in the nineteenth century when the lower Rio Grande Valley was settled on a large scale.

Another sectional distinction was the use of jacal construction in mountainous areas on both sides of the Rio Grande Valley. As used in the nineteenth century, jacal is very different from that of the ancient Pueblos. Much sturdier, it made use of large posts (5 to 8 inches in diameter) set contiguously in deep trenches and sharpened in a wedge shape at their upper ends (fig. 71). These were fitted into a groove on the bottom side of a heavy horizontal log which capped the vertical logs and held them in uniform positions. Though resting on vertical poles, this horizontal plate was also supported by still heavier forked posts placed at each corner. The plate supported vigas which carried the usual flat roof covered with earth; it could also support rafters of a ridge roof if such were added above the flat roof to deflect rain. Although no wattle is employed to weave the upright members together, the heavy log walls were plastered with mud to make them weathertight. The introduction of doors and windows caused no special problems in such construction, but fireplaces or iron stoves were restricted to freestanding positions in the interior. This late form resembles the "poteaux-en-terre" French construction in the Mississippi Valley. Knowledge of it could have been brought into New Mexico in the early nineteenth century by French trappers, but substantial jacal walls were also constructed by colonial builders.

While discussing local differences, it is appropriate to mention Gothic Revival designs which offered the sole alternative to Territorial style. Found only on churches, this version of the revival, which should really be designated as "Folk Gothic" or "Gothick" to differentiate its absurd if rather delightful

71 Jacal construction of the late nineteenth century employed large posts embedded in the ground and trimmed at the top to fit into a channeled plate. Walls of jacal and adobe were frequently used in the same building.

attempts to recall the manner of the Middle Ages, was favored by Bishop Lamy (fig. 72). He and his coworkers, many of whom were also French, seem to have included the renovation of church art and architecture along with general ecclesiastical reforms. They appear to have regarded the traditional religious sculpture and painting of the region as uncouth, if not blasphemous, and the simple mud churches as unworthy houses of worship. At the earliest possible opportunity they sought to replace them with buildings and works of art more worthy of the name "Christian." It is our good fortune, however, that parish finances usually precluded the erection of new, rather mundane structures of stone like the Cathedral in Santa Fe or the church of Our Lady of Sorrows in Las Vegas; much more interesting is the icing of wooden Gothick shapes which sought to disguise the old adobe fabric. Good examples of these are found in Albuquerque, Bernalillo, and in Isleta Pueblo—the last, lamentably, now "re-restored" in the Pueblo style with concrete block towers. Gothic or even Gothic Revival, of course, these buildings are not, but there is about them a sincerity and ingenuousness which command sympathy if not emulation (figs. 73, 74). They occupy a unique position in architectural history; nowhere else in the world will one find this particular combination of adobe construction and wooden Gothick veneer.

72   San Felipe church and rectory, Albuquerque. The building, erected about 1790, was modernized with wooden trim in 1876–80 by Jesuits then assigned to the church. Photograph, 1881, by Ben Wittick.

73 Details of the "Gothick" trim executed in wood.

74 San Agustin church, Isleta Pueblo; built before 1629, "Gothicized" about 1880. Photograph before the 1960 restoration.

Although the Territorial style was outmoded in trading centers along the railroad after 1880 by new fashions in building, it hung on in isolated mountain villages of northern New Mexico. There, in the hands of anonymous carpenter-builders, the old style developed as a folk art and produced what is probably its most charming expression. Completely innocent of ancient prototypes which had inspired the Greek Revival on the east coast, these craftsmen copied, improvised on, and modified the handful of Classical details that had found their way into New Mexico a generation earlier. As in all folk art there were no fundamental innovations, no ideas that were original or revolutionary; instead there was infinite variation on a few decorative themes, as the doors pictured here will indicate (figs. 75, 76).

These folk artists, whose names are sometimes not even known, worked in isolation, each in his own village; but often a man's work can be identified by his decorative vocabulary and manner of composing, and perhaps by a repeated use

75 Folk Territorial doors of the Policarpio Romero house, Peñasco. Now installed in the chapel at Los Luceros, these were made by Gregorio Ortega about 1870.

76   Folk Territorial door from Llano de San Juan, about 1910.

of certain tools. It is important to realize that though they were well supplied with ample quantities of sawn lumber and good hand tools, these artists still cut moldings by hand, using beautiful block planes, a different one for each profile. As these planes were relatively expensive, the number possessed by a given carpenter was limited and hence so was his repertoire of moldings. Although much is yet to be learned about this topic, the work of several craftsmen has been identified, including that of Gregorio Ortega of Truchas who worked in the 1870s. Later practitioners, who worked into the 1900s, were Alejandro Gallegos of Peñasco and Aniceto Garduño of Chacon. Most of these carpenters also made furniture.

The longevity of this folk art tradition, which lasted as long as the villages remained isolated, is fascinating. For months during the winter these localities were virtually inaccessible, and even in good weather the means of transportation was too limited to haul in anything as bulky as factory-made doors or windows. Thus, manufacture was left to the local carpenter. This condition, romantic and sociologically healthy in many ways, only changed after World War I. About the same time numbers of wealthy outsiders began to move to Santa Fe and Taos where they discovered this folk art along with examples of the colonial period. Several of this group, among them Cyrus McCormick of Chicago, purchased old architectural elements to incorporate in new homes they were building with the result that the best examples of this folk art remaining today are found in such dwellings, not in the villages.

5

The railroad reached Las Vegas in 1879, Santa Fe and Albuquerque a year later. It brought New Mexico into the mainstream of American culture and resulted in a flood of American architectural fashions that were or had been in current use in the eastern United States. A wide selection of building materials and manufactured items, available to New Mexican builders for the first time was also conducive to change. That there was a transformation in architecture after 1880 is not surprising, but this change was largely confined to communities with access to the railroad. Remote villages were hardly affected. Mining towns were the exception; they were largely controlled by Americans who thought progress was synonymous with what could be imported from the States. Inasmuch as miners had to provide good transportation to get their ore to market, they possessed the facilities to haul building products back from the railway depot.

The new materials that caused this revolution were varied: cast iron columns for store fronts; pressed metal cornices and window heads which, when painted, resembled more costly carved stone; whole façades of pressed metal; corrugated iron roofing as a substitute for terneplate or shingles; factory-made windows, doors, trim, and moldings; hardwood, to supplement New Mexico pine, for floors or fancy woodwork; brick in great variety of color and size (though after 1879 New Mexico produced brick of its own); cement and plaster to supplant mud surfaces; window glass in larger size; iron stoves and furnaces; and eventually gas and plumbing fixtures.

Once the new materials and the up-to-date fashions arrived, New Mexico towns rapidly lost their regional imprint and began to resemble any small town in the Midwest. Sometimes, as at Santa Fe, the new wave of building was

108

imposed on the old order, for the time being almost engulfing it. In instances where the railroad did not touch the existing community, as in Albuquerque or to some extent Las Vegas, a separate railroad town grew up adjacent to the tracks to challenge the old center, which soon surrendered its commercial importance but retained vestiges of its early appearance. In the present study our only interest in this new expression is to illustrate how rapidly the technology of the area was transformed and how this modified the region's architecture. New Mexico offers a laboratory in which architectural and technological change may be correlated.

To chronicle subsequent changes in American architectural fashions as they were domesticated in New Mexico would take another book. It will suffice to mention a couple of phenomena which may be unique in American history. The railroad brought a bewildering assortment of architectural styles: Italianate-Bracketed, Mansard, Queen Anne, Richardson Romanesque, and before long Colonial Revival and Worlds Fair Classic. These styles arrived all at once and they competed for public acceptance on an equal basis. Italianate was considered quite as up-to-date as Queen Anne, though in the East the former had been discarded for more than a decade before the latter was "invented." But since few New Mexicans had any notion of what easterners considered fashionable, the thing that mattered to them was that both manners were fresh from the States and therefore desirable. The consequent mix-up in stylistic sequence is illustrated by four New Mexico mansions built within a four-year period: Huning Castle in Albuquerque, an "Italian Villa" constructed in 1881 of adobe and veneered with wood; the castleated Dorsey mansion, begun in 1880, on a ranch east of Springer; the Mills mansion in Springer, also from 1880, surrounded by the traditional New Mexican two-story verandah but capped with a mansard roof; and the Preston-Polemus house in Santa Fe, a good Queen Anne design, up-to-date by any standards for 1883 (figs. 77, 78).

Chronological confusion also results from the overlap of two phases of Classical revivalism, the Territorial and the Worlds Fair Classic. The latter, pioneered by McKim, Mead, and White, and others in the late 1880s, and popularized by the Columbian Exposition in 1893, reached territorial centers like Albuquerque about 1900. At the same time, the folk version of the Territorial style, which descended from the Greek Revival of the 1830s, still thrived in mountain villages. Thus separate phases of Classicism, of quite diverse historical derivation, flourished simultaneously.

A comparable mix-up occurs about the same time when the *surviving* Spanish-Pueblo manner ran parallel to a *revival* of the same tradition. The former had been maintained in Indian pueblos with the construction of churches like that at Santo Domingo in 1890. By 1907, the newly founded university in Albuquerque turned to such puebloid forms as flat roofs and projecting vigas when remodeling a classroom building (figs. 79, 80). In 1917, the state

77 The Dorsey mansion, northeast of Springer, 1878–81; a thirty-six-room stone and log dwelling built in a "medieval" style. Photograph by Robert Nugent.

78 Huning Castle, Albuquerque, 1881. This adobe structure with an Italian Villa wood veneer was the finest nineteenth-century mansion in New Mexico. Demolished 1955.

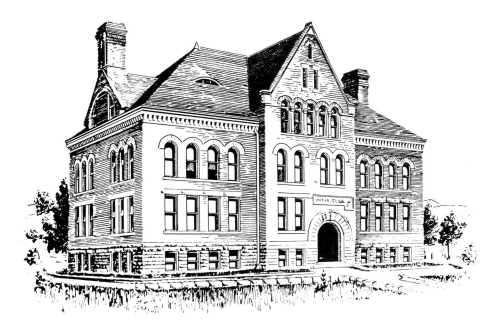

79 Hodgin (formerly University) Hall, University of New Mexico, Albuquerque. This structure of brick and sandstone was designed in the Richardson Romanesque manner in 1890, one year after the university was founded.

government built an approximate replica of the Acoma church for its art museum in Santa Fe (fig. 81). The revival is known as the Santa Fe style.

This phase of simultaneous revival and survival of an architectural style provides a key to understanding New Mexico architecture—an eclectic architecture based on different cultural influences and responsive to technological innovations reliant on the practicalities of trade patterns. If nothing else, New Mexico architecture has been—and will probably always be—unique.

80 Hodgin Hall as remodeled in the Spanish Pueblo or Santa Fe style in 1909.

81   The Museum of New Mexico, Santa Fe, revived Pueblo style.

SOURCES OF ILLUSTRATIONS

Perry Borchers, Ohio State University: 35
Roy Boyd: 41
John Ellin, Albuquerque: 71
Dick Kent, Albuquerque: 9, 10
Arthur LaZar, Albuquerque: 1, 47, 49, 56, 65, 66, 69, 75
Rowena Martínez, Taos: 60
Robert Nugent, 77
Ewing Waterhouse, El Paso: 76

Historic American Building Survey: 38, 45, 48, 62
Museum of New Mexico, Photographic Archives: 70
National Archives, Washington, D.C.: 9, 19, 21, 50, 26, 56, 63, 70
New Mexico Tourist Office: 68, 74
Smithsonian Institution National Anthropological Archives: 4, 5, 27, 28, 32, 33, 34, 23

B. Bunting and William Sims. *Taos Adobes* (Santa Fe: Museum of New Mexico, 1964): 51, 64
Neil M. Judd. "The Architecture of Pueblo Boni-to," Smithsonian Institution, Miscellaneous Collections Volume 147, no. 1 (Washington, D.C., 1964): 6, 8
Victor Mindeleff. "A Study of Pueblo Architecture in Tusayan and Cibola," Smithsonian Institution, Eighth Annual Report of the Bureau of American Ethnology (Washington, D.C., 1891): 16, 18, 20, 24, 25, 29, 30, 31
New Mexico Architecture 2 (Sept. 1960): 72
Frank H. H. Roberts. "The Ruins at Kiatuthlanna in Eastern Arizona," Smithsonian Institution, Bureau of American Ethnology Bulletin 100 (Washington, D.C., 1931): 14
Gordon Vivian and T. W. Mathews. "Kin Kletso, A Pueblo III Community," Southwest Parks and Monuments Association Volume 6, part 1 (Denver, 1973): 5
H. M. Wormington. *Prehistoric Indians of the Southwest* (Denver: Colorado Museum of Natural History, 1947): 24

All other illustrations by the author

BIBLIOGRAPHY

A complete history of the architecture of New Mexico is yet to be written and, indeed, such an effort at this point would be premature. The reasons for this condition are many: the disappearance of a discouragingly high percentage of the early buildings; a paucity of documentation; a scarcity of firm information based on archaeological investigations of early Spanish sites; and a shortage of studies focusing on a specific building or community which normally furnish the "building blocks" out of which a more comprehensive history is constructed. The present work, a kind of practice run, is an attempt to outline building activity in the region from aboriginal to almost modern times, but it poses as many questions as it provides answers. However, by describing a problem, hypothesizing a relationship, or nominating a "first" example, others are challenged to probe and question and thereby to unearth the needed facts from which an authoritative account can be written.

The following bibliography and notes make no attempt to be complete; rather they are intended to direct the student to sources representing a variety of approaches to the topic. Reflecting the limits imposed on the book, they are restricted to buildings of the pre–World War I era.

INDIAN ARCHITECTURE

Information pertaining to Indian architecture for the most part must be ferreted out from archaeological reports. To the architect it may appear that archaeologists seldom treat architecture as an end in itself but as one more component in that enormously complex assortment of data from which a picture of a given culture can be reconstructed. With importance given to every stone, sherd, and artifact, and the context in which each was found, it is not surprising that the general reader is sometimes overwhelmed by the detail and statistics of the average excavation report in which it may be difficult to see the proverbial forest for the trees.

In many ways the most illuminating treatment of early Indian architecture of the Southwest is the first one written: Victor Mindeleff, "A Study of Pueblo Architecture of Tusayan and Cibola."

Based on material gathered during four extended field trips between 1881 and 1888, it was published as the *Eighth Annual Report* of the Bureau of Ethnology in 1891. This long article which has superb plans and line drawings, describes the architecture of Zuñi and Hopi villages at a time when their building tradition had still not been too much affected by American or even Spanish technology. It was also written before living pueblos were closed to examination and photography by outsiders. Although a few assumptions made by this pioneer investigator have been invalidated by later findings, this hardly diminishes the value of the architectural data contained in the book.

For the beginner a good introduction to prehistoric Indian culture of the area is furnished by an old but reliable work: H. Marie Wormington, *Prehistoric Indians of the Southwest* (Denver: Colorado Museum of Natural History, 1947). More recent and detailed is Gordon Willey, *An Introduction to American Archaeology: North America* (Englewood Cliffs, N.J.: Prentice Hall, 1966). Also readable and well-illustrated are sections in H. S. Gladwin, *History of the Ancient Southwest* (Portland, Maine: Bond-Wheelwright, 1957). Although several fundamental hypotheses proposed by this author have not found acceptance among anthropologists, this does not seriously affect the architectural discussion. Recommended also because it deals with architecture in terms of social artifact is Paul Martin and Fred Plog, *The Archaeology of Arizona* (New York: American Museum of Natural History, 1973).

For the beginner another good way to grasp the evolution of Pueblo architecture is to read about one site that enjoyed several periods of occupancy. Such reports by one of the most readable anthropologists, Frank H. H. Roberts, are "The Ruins at Kiathuthlanna," Smithsonian Institution, Bureau of American Ethnology Bulletin 92 (Washington, D.C., 1929) and "Shabik' eschee Village," Smithsonian Institution, Bureau of American Ethnology Bulletin 100 (Washington, D.C., 1931). Roberts also summarizes the sequence in "Development of the Unit-Type Dwelling," in the Hewett Anniversary Album, *So Live the Works of Man* (Albuquerque: University of New Mexico Press, 1939). For the development of kivas there are two useful studies: Florence Hawley, "Big Kivas, Little Kivas, and Moiety Houses," *Southwestern Journal of Anthropology* 6:286–302, and Gordon Vivian and Paul Reiter, "The Great Kivas of Chaco Canyon and Their Relationships," School of American Research Monograph 22 (Santa Fe, 1960).

An exhaustive study of what is probably the most important single prehistoric structure in the Southwest was made by Neil M. Judd, *Architecture of Pueblo Bonito*, Smithsonian Institution, Miscellaneous Collection, Volume 147 no. 1 (Washington, D.C., 1964). But this classic reference is so packed with fact that a nonspecialist may have difficulty identifying the generalizations and conclusions. Early studies on Spruce Tree House and Cliff Palace ruins at Mesa Verde by Jesse Fewkes, who restored these cliff dwellings for the National Park Service, are disappointingly brief. These studies appeared as Bureau of American Ethnology Bulletins 41 and 51 (Washington, D.C., 1909 and 1911). In a popular vein Don Watson has written several books on that area: *Indians of the Mesa Verde* and *Cliff Dwellings of the Mesa Verde, A Story in Pictures*, both published in 1961 for the Mesa Verde Museum Association. An interesting article on the possible relationships between prehistoric architecture of the Four Corners area, southern Arizona, and Central Mexico is Edwin N. Ferndon, *A Trial Survey of Mexican-Southwestern Parallels*, School of American Research Monograph 22 (Santa Fe, 1955).

A serious obstacle to an understanding of contemporary pueblo architecture is the reluctance of present-day Indians to permit photography or examination of their communities. Information relating architecture of historic times, therefore, is largely confined to ruins or to pueblos as they existed before World War I. About the only way one presently has to photograph some contemporary communities is from the air, as Stanley Stubbs did in *Bird's Eye View of the Pueblos*

(Norman: University of Oklahoma Press, 1950). Or one may speculate about them in environmental terms as Vincent Scully did in *Pueblo, Mountain, Village, Dance* (New York: Viking, 1975), a highly personal interpretation of the orientation of pueblos in relation to their topographical setting.

SPANISH COLONIAL AND EARLY AMERICAN ARCHITECTURE

Literature on Spanish Colonial architecture of the Southwest is spotty. Of paramount importance among the scanty primary sources is Fray Francisco Atanasio Domínguez, *The Missions of New Mexico, 1776,* translated and edited by Eleanor B. Adams and Fray Angelico Chavez (Albuquerque: University of New Mexico Press, 1956). This detailed description and inventory was made by a meticulous church official sent from Mexico to inspect the missions. A reprint of this work (Albuquerque: University of New Mexico Press, 1976) has been published and an accompanying volume illustrating the missions as they exist today is projected for 1977 as part of the American Bicentennial commemoration. The "Last Will and Testament of Severino Martínez," translated and annotated by Ward Alan Minge (*New Mexico Quarterly* 33:33–56), provides an insight into the material limitations of the area and the practice of dividing a large house among several heirs. The best political history of the area is M. E. Jenkins and A. H. Schroeder, *Brief History of New Mexico* (Albuquerque: University of New Mexico Press, 1974).

A well-written, popular introduction to colonial building in this region is provided by Trent Sanford, *Architecture of the Southwest* (New York: W. W. Norton, 1950; later edition, 1971) who summarizes early New Mexican building and compares it with that of Texas, Arizona, and California. The sole authoritative study on one aspect of the topic is George Kubler, *The Religious Architecture of New Mexico* (Colorado Springs: Colorado Springs Fine Arts Center, 1941; reissued in 1974 by the University of New Mexico Press). Kubler's bibliography and footnotes thoroughly canvass known sources, and his text leaves nothing to add except a few supplementary notes pertaining to nineteenth-century examples. Volumes on the same topic by Bradford Prince, Reginald Fisher, and Earl R. Forrest contain little that is not found in Kubler. Architecture of the morada, a type of religious building, is discussed in Richard Ahlborn, *The Penitente Moradas of Abiquiu*, Smithsonian Institution, Contributions from the Museums of History and Technology Paper 63 (Washington, D.C., 1968).

No comprehensive treatment of colonial vernacular architecture exists. The most eminent authority of Spanish Colonial art, the late E. Boyd, Curator of Spanish Colonial Art for the Museum of New Mexico, included a chapter on domestic architecture in her incomparable *Popular Arts of Spanish New Mexico* (Santa Fe: Museum of New Mexico Press, 1974). On domestic architecture there are several small volumes: Sytha Motto, *Old Houses of New Mexico and the People Who Built Them* (Albuquerque: Calvin Horn Publisher, 1972); Bainbridge Bunting, *Taos Adobes* (Santa Fe: Museum of New Mexico, 1964); Bainbridge Bunting and Arthur LaZar, *Of Earth and Timber Built,* (Albuquerque: University of New Mexico Press, 1974). But none of these is conclusive. The first is stronger on family association and anecdote than on architecture or documentation; the second summarizes the characteristics and technology of colonial building but deals with only a limited geographical area; and the last, though it contains some interesting insights and facts, is primarily a book of handsome photographs.

Regional periodicals contain information on architecture. An early publication (1913–16) entitled *Old Santa Fe* contained two important articles: W. H. H. Allison, "Santa Fe as It Appeared During the Years 1837–38," *Old Santa Fe* 2:170–83, and Sylvanus Morley, "Santa Fe Architecture," *Old Santa Fe* 2:278–301. More recently *New Mexico Architecture,* sponsored by the state chapter of the American Institute of Architecture, has featured articles on historic architecture. Aside from more than a dozen short articles on individual buildings are three of somewhat greater breadth by B. Bunting and John Conron: "The Architecture of the Embudo Watershed" (4, no. 5:19–27); "The Architecture of Northern New Mexico" (8, no. 9:14–49); and "Guide to the Architecture of Northern New Mexico" (12, no. 7, entire issue). The last by John Conron and Bainbridge Bunting, was compiled as a guide for the annual tour of the Society of Architectural Historians which visited the state in 1970. Also notable in the same publication are two articles by David Gebhard entitled "Architecture and the Fred Harvey Houses" (4, no. 7:11–17 and 6, no. 1:18–25). *El Palacio,* published by the Museum of New Mexico since 1913, from time to time has contained articles of architectural interest. Of particular note are: "The Lost Pecos Church," by B. T. Ellis, S. A. Stubbs, and A. E. Dittert (64, no. 3:67–92); E. Boyd, "Fireplaces and Stoves in Colonial New Mexico" (65, no. 6:219–24); J. J. Brody and Anne Colberg, "A Spanish Homestead near Placitas, N.M." (73, no. 2:11–20); and entire issues devoted to Adobe (77, no. 4), Historic Preservation (78, no. 2), and the Palace of the Governors (80, no. 3). The *New Mexico Historical Review* tends toward biographical, political, and military subjects, but sometimes includes information on military architecture: J. M. Foster, Jr., "Fort Bascomb" (35: 30–62); R. M. Utley, "Fort Union and the Santa Fe Trail" (36: 36–48); Max Moorhead, "Presidio Supply Problems in New Mexico in the 18th Century" (36:210–29); T. J. Warner, "Frontier Defense" (41: 5–19); Frank McNitt, "Fort Sumner" (45: 101–17); and Max Moorhead, "Rebuilding the Presidio of Santa Fe, 1789–91" (49: 123–42).

Two volumes on the architecture of a single community have been published. *Old Santa Fe Today* (Santa Fe: School of American Research, 1966 and 1972) is well documented, handsomely produced, and can be used as a guide book; it covers buildings of all periods. On a more modest scale is Charles L. Nieman, *Spanish Times and Boom Times, Toward an Architectural History of Socorro* (Socorro: Socorro County Historical Society, 1972).

Unpublished studies undertaken pursuant to academic degrees are mines of information. Some of these include Richard Ahlborn, "Spanish Colonial Woodcarving in New Mexico, 1598–1841" (M.A. thesis, University of Delaware, 1958); Louise Harris, "Art and Architecture of Srampas, N.M." (M.A. thesis, University of New Mexico, 1967); Louise Harris Ivers, "The Architecture of Las Vegas, N.M." (Ph.D. dissertation, University of New Mexico, 1975); and Charles F. Gritzner, "Spanish Log Construction in New Mexico" (Ph.D. dissertation, Louisiana State University, 1969). Some material from the last title appeared as "Log Housing in New Mexico," *Pioneer America* 2, no. 2: 54–62.

Finally a good deal of architectural information can be derived from diaries and travel accounts written by merchants, officials, and military persons who visited New Mexico after American penetration into the area. These are particularly useful for domestic architecture for which little documentation and few photographs exist. A digest of these travel accounts is contained in John P. Bloom, "New Mexico Viewed by Anglo-Americans," *New Mexico Historical Review* 34: 165–98. Worthy of particular mention among these are: J. W. Abert, "Report of His Examination of New Mexico in the Years 1846–47" (Senate Executive Doc. 23, 30th Cong. First Sess., 1848); Susan S. Magoffin, *Down the Santa Fe Trail and Into Mexico, 1846–47* (New Haven: Yale University Press, 1926); and *Matt Field on the Santa Fe Trail,* edited by J. E. Sunder (Norman: University of Oklahoma Press, 1960). The last, an engaging series of articles about a trip in 1839, written for the *New Orleans Picayune,* contains a good description of early trading forts and of Ranchos de Taos as a walled town.

Finally a note is in order concerning available archival resources. In New Mexico deeds and tax records, a usual source of information in other parts of the country, are often incomplete or nonexistent, a condition that derives in part from carelessness with which official records were handled during the transition from Mexican to American administrations. The possibilities of research have been enormously improved, however, since the activation in 1960 of the New Mexico Records Center in Santa Fe in which surviving records were put in order and placed in safety; an effort was also made to locate documents that had disappeared. Tax records of counties constituted since American annexation have been collected and put on microfilm there. With a catalog, and especially with the help of the dedicated staff, one can now locate such information as survives. Equally important, the Archives of the Archdiocese of Santa Fe have been recorded on microfilm, and scholars now have access to them at the University of New Mexico library. One other very important source of information for buildings of a given locality during the Territorial period are the newspapers. Most of these are available on microfilm at the University of New Mexico library.

Facilities for research, sometimes very complete within a specific field, exist at the School of American Research in Santa Fe, the Fort Burgwin Research Center in Taos, the Special Collections of the University of New Mexico Library, the Special Collections of the Museum of New Mexico in Santa Fe, the Old Santa Fe Association, and the Albuquerque Landmarks Commission at the Museum of Albuquerque. The Office of Historic Preservation established in recent years within the State Planning Office in Santa Fe also has become an important repository where one can find information relating to buildings and sites that have been designated a National Monument, a Historic Site, or placed on the Cultural Properties list of the state.

Cataloging and rounding out of holdings of the Photographic Archives of the Museum of New Mexico, thanks to the concerted effort of the staff and administration, have greatly enhanced our knowledge of the region's early architecture. The photographic collections of several other institutions have also been increased, sometimes by the sensible expedient of copying rare views. Additional collections are held by the University of New Mexico, the Albuquerque Public Library, the Museum of Albuquerque, the Socorro County Historical Society, and several individuals. The last few years have also witnessed new interest in early photographers who worked in the Southwest. Books on them include: Beaumont Newhall and Diana Edkin, *William H. Jackson* (Dobbs Ferry: Morgan and Morgan, 1974); Gar and Maggy Packard, *Southwest in 1880 with Ben Wittick, Pioneer Photographer,* (Santa Fe: Packard and Packard, 1970); *Adam Clark Vroman, Photographer of the Southwest,* edited by Ruth Mahood (Los Angeles: Ward-Richie Press, 1961); and J. D. McKee and Spencer Wilson, *Socorro Photographer: Joseph Edward Smith* (Socorro: Socorro County Historical Society, 1974).

INDEX

Ft. Union, 5, 98
Ft. Wingate, 5, 38
foundations, building, 8
Franciscans, 3, 4, 35, 87
Frijoles Canyon, ruins, 15, 27

Gallegos, Alejandro, 107
Garduño, Aniceto, 107
Gibson, Lt. George, 69
Giusewa Pueblo, 58
Gran Quivira, 58, 75
grist mills, 82, 85
Gritzner, Charles, 85

haciendas, 60
Halona Pueblo, 32, 51, 58
hardware, 4, 5, 69, 71, 74
Hillers, John K., 31, 32, 35, 37
Hopi pueblos, 27, 30, 37, 41, 47
hornos. *See* ovens
house plans, 60, 63–65, 80, 90
houses. *See* architecture, domestic
Humanas. *See* Gran Quivira

Indians: Apache, 30, 35, 54, 96; Basket Maker, 17–20
    passim; Hopi, 27, 30, 37, 41, 47; hostilities, 3, 4, 29, 30,
    54, 86, 88, 90, 96, 100; Navajo, 6, 30, 35, 37, 96;
    prehistoric, 1–4 passim; Pueblo, 2–3, 19; Pueblo
    Revolt of 1680, 3, 4, 30, 32, 81; Western Apache, 35;
    Zuñi, 27, 30, 31–35, 67, 75
Isleta Pueblo, 27, 30, 58, 102

jacal. *See* walls, jacal
Jemez Pueblo, 58
Jesuits in N.M., 5
Jews in N.M., 6

Kearny, Stephen Watts, 5
Kin Kletso ruins, 27, 29
Kin Tiel ruins, 27, 37
kivas, 20, 21, 22–23, 29, 35

La Ciénega, 82
ladders, 19, 22, 26, 29, 30, 37
Laguna Pueblo, 30, 59
Lamy, Jean Baptiste, 4, 5, 86, 87, 102
land grants, 52, 53, 54
Las Golondrinas Ranch, 82
Las Trampas, 4, 54, 59, 63, 82
Las Truchas, 82, 107
Las Vegas, 63, 94, 95, 108; Presbyterian church, 96; Our
    Lady of Sorrows, 102, 108, 109
Long, Horace, 71
Los Luceros, 90

McKim, Mead, and White, 109
Martínez, Antonio Severino, 63, 80
masonry. *See* walls
mealing bins, 43
Mesa Verde ruins, 21, 26
metal, pressed, 95, 108
Mexico: administration of N.M., 4, 5, 87; War of
    Independence, 5, 87

mill sawn lumber. *See* boards, mill sawn
mill work. *See* wood trim
Mills mansion, 109
Mindeleff, Victor, 31, 32, 35, 38, 41, 43, 47, 50, 75
mural decoration, 41, 58

New Mexico: agriculture, 53; economy of, 3, 5, 6, 7, 30,
    53–54, 86, 87; mining, 6, 54, 88; occupied by U.S.
    troops, 5; statehood, 6; Taos rebellion of 1846, 29;
    Territorial period, 5, 6
Nusbaum, Gus, 31

oblique windows, 41
Ojo Caliente, 54
Oñate, Juan de, 54
Ortega, Gregorio, 107
O'Sullivan, Timothy, 31
out buildings, 28, 82
ovens, 37, 43, 59

parapets, 37, 94, 100
Pecos, 1, 56, 101
Peñasco, 107
Penitentes, 5
photographs of early N.M., 31, 90, 98
Picuris Pueblo, 10, 59
piki oven, 43
pintle door, 38
pithouses, 17, 19, 26
placita, 60
plaster interiors, 72
population, 2, 3, 22, 52, 55, 87
portal, 72, 90, 94, 95, 100
portico, 96
portón, 71
poteaux-en-terre, 101
Powell, David, 96
puddled adobe, 9–10, 27
Pueblo Bonito ruins, 22–26, 29, 32

Quarai ruins, 58, 75

railroads, 6, 30, 31, 86, 87, 108–9
Ranchos de Taos, 59, 63, 71
Roman Catholic church: architectural activity under
    Lamy, 96, 102; reorganization under Lamy, 5, 86, 87;
    support of missions, 3, 4
roof construction, 8, 14; American, 94, 100, 101; Indian,
    17, 19, 23, 25, 41; Spanish, 65
roof hatchways, 19, 20–22, 26, 29, 40–41, 82

San Antonio, Tex., Governor's Palace, 80
San Felipe Pueblo, 30
San Gabriel ruins, 52
San Juan Pueblo, 52
San Miguel del Vado, 63, 88
Santa Ana, 8
Santa Clara, 59
Santa Cruz, 4, 59
Santa Fe, 6, 52, 53, 59, 81, 94, 95, 108; Art Museum, 109;
    cathedral, 102; Federal Building, 80, 100; Ft. Marcy,
    96, 98; Palace of the Governors, 1, 54, 65, 69, 80–81,
    82, 88, 100; plaza, 90; Preston-Polemus house, 109